Contents

Page		
2	Introduction	
3	"No Place for Children in a War: The World War II Stories of Noel Streatfeild	Harriet Jordan
14	Geoffrey Trease and "The Toughest Fight Ever": Passion versus Balance	Sally Dore
21	The Twins Books of Lucy Fitch Perkins	Clarissa Cridland
27	"Don't Mention the War"	Ruth Allen
32	Angela Brazil's Wartime Books as Socio-historical Documents	Sarah Burn
41	Feisty Girls in the Books of C. Bernard Rutley	Kay Whalley
48	Writing about War – Authors' Experiences Helen Barber, Katherine Bruce, Sheena Wilkinson	
56	War, Eric Linklater and The Wind on the Moon	Elizabeth Williams
65	Girls of the Great War: A Picture in Words and Music	
81	What Were Schoolgirls Reading in 1918?	Sally Dore
92	"Me, Louise Plewes, and the Anne Digby Mystery	Louise Plewes
98	Clare Mallory: The Person Behind the Pseudonym	Barbara Robertson
108	What Can a Girl Do In Wartime? The Books of Rosemary Sutcliff	Julia McLaughlin Cook
114	Wartime Aviatrixes: Worrals and Marise	Stephen Bigger
121	Wartime Schools: The Chalet School and Dora Joan Potter's Winterton Series	Katherine Bruce
130	Entertaining Evacuees	Sue Sims
136	Book Launch: Career Novels for Girls	Kay Clifford
137	Books set in Wartime: Recommended Reading	

Introduction

The Sixth Bristol Conference
Wills Hall, 27th -29th July 2018

Our sixth conference, like the previous five, was friendly, entertaining, and full of erudition. Wills Hall (one of the University of Bristol's halls of residence) again proved a splendid venue for our gathering, which had the biggest number of participants yet, including to our delight more than ten per cent from overseas.

Our first thanks must go to all our speakers who informed and entertained us so wonderfully. We are extremely fortunate that such knowledgeable and entertaining people are willing to share their enthusiasm and expertise in this way. To mark the centenary of the ending of World War I in 1918, the overall theme of the conference was war in various guises, but as usual we had a splendidly wide variety of subjects, approaches and styles. Our speakers have also kindly agreed to their papers being published in this book. The order of papers in this book reflects the order in which they were delivered at the conference, with the Saturday evening entertainment in the middle, so as it give the same experience of variety our conference-goers experienced.

We'd also like to thank all the conference-goers who helped in so many ways over the weekend, particularly those who chaired sessions. And a very large measure of thanks and appreciation go to our respective families, without whom running these conferences would not be possible. (And to Alexander for help with proof-reading.)

Looking forward to 2020, our seventh conference will be held from the 24th July – 26th / 27th July 2020, so do make a note in your diaries now. The linking theme will be Misfits, Oddballs and Eccentrics although as usual we will have a wide range of presentations. Details of the conference and how to book for it will be on the Topsy-Turvy web-site at the end of July 2019. The address is:
http://www.topsyturvychildrensbooks.co.uk
We hope to see you there!

Betula O'Neill and Sally Dore

"No Place for Children in a War": The World War II Stories of Noel Streatfeild
Harriet Jordan

The theme of the 2018 Bristol Conference being War, one of the areas the organisers wanted to explore was authors who had written about war both contemporaneously and retrospectively. In this presentation, I will be considering the difference between war as background, and war as story, in the works of Noel Streatfeild. I will be looking at her depiction of World War II, and how this differs between the contemporary and historical books.

Noel Streatfeild lived through both World Wars. Born in 1895, during World War I she worked in the kitchen at a hospital for wounded soldiers, and then in a munitions factory. After the war she trained and worked as an actress, before giving up the stage to become an author in 1929. By 1939 she had published seven adult novels and four children's books, including the one for which she is best known, *Ballet Shoes*. During World War II she worked for the Women's Voluntary Service, while continuing to write for both children and adults. After the war she wrote fewer adult novels, but was increasingly prolific as a writer for children. In the 1970s she began writing historical children's books, including the World War II story *When the Siren Wailed*. She died in 1986.

Noel Streatfeild wrote two books with a World War I background, the adult novel *Parson's Nine* (1932), and *Goodbye to the Maitlands*, an unpublished children's story from the 1980s. Below are her books written during or about the Second World War (the romances as Susan Scarlett).

Novels	Romances	Children's books
The Winter is Past (1940)	*Peter and Paul* (1940)	*The House in Cornwall* (1940)
I Ordered a Table for Six (1942)	*Ten-Way Street* (1940)	*The Children of Primrose Lane* (1941)
Myra Carroll (1944)	*The Man in the Dark* (1941)	*Harlequinade* (1943)
Saplings (1945)	*Babbacombe's* (1941)	*Curtain Up* (1944)
Beyond the Vicarage (1971) [fictionalised autobiography]	*Under the Rainbow* (1942)	*Party Frock* (1946)
	Summer Pudding (1943)	*When the Siren Wailed* (1974)
	Murder While You Work (1944)	

I will be concentrating on four books set during World War II:
- *The Children of Primrose Lane* - six children capture a German spy
- *Curtain Up* - a family of three children move to London and attend The Children's Academy of Dancing and Stage Training (somewhat changed since *Ballet Shoes*)

- *Party Frock* - a family of children in a village put on a pageant to provide an occasion for their cousin to wear a party frock she has been sent by her American godmother
- *When the Siren Wailed* - a family of three Cockney children is evacuated from London to a village in the country

I won't be looking at *The House in Cornwall* (which doesn't appear to be set during the war) or *Harlequinade* (which is more of a mood piece).

The historical work, *When the Siren Wailed*, offers a chronicle of the war, presenting and explaining a world readers are not familiar with. By contrast, the three contemporary books are relating people's lived experience: war is an ever-present background, but not something that needs to be explained, because readers are still experiencing it (at the time of publication of *Primrose Lane* and *Curtain Up*), or would still have clear memories (when *Party Frock* was published). To examine this, I will be looking at various aspects of the war, to see how they are treated differently in the contemporary and the historical books.

Context

When looking at these books and their relationship to World War II, it is important to understand what was happening at the time the books were written. The timeline below shows the key events of the war, with a number of periods highlighted: the Phoney war, when war had been declared, but there was no significant military action; the Battle of Britain, where the German Luftwaffe attacked British airfields, ports and shipping centres; the Blitz period of night-time bombing of London; and the second period of intense London bombing, this time using the V-1 flying bombs. Below the timeline are the periods covered by each of the four books. *The Children of Primrose Lane* was written during the Blitz, when the author was suffering through night-time bombing, and working for the Women's Voluntary Service. It takes place in 1940, after the Dunkirk evacuation, but probably during the Battle of Britain rather than the Blitz. *Curtain Up* (later reprinted as *Theatre Shoes*) was published in 1944, and so written before the V-1 bombing began. It is set in London, and takes place after the Blitz, when people – including children - were beginning to return to the capital. It finishes in December 1943, so neither the characters nor the author were aware that six months later bombs would again be raining down on London. *Party Frock*, written not long after the war ended, runs from December 1944 to September 1945, and incorporates the surrender of the German forces in Europe, and then of the Japanese forces in the Pacific.

When the Siren Wailed covers a much longer time period than the contemporary books, beginning with the issuing of gas masks before the war, and finishing in summer 1943. Most of the events in the book take place during the time of the Phoney War, the Battle of Britain and the Blitz.

World Events

These four books contain very little reference to events outside Britain. The Dunkirk evacuation in mentioned in passing in *Primrose Lane* ('*I fought in Norway, and I was brought back from Dunkirk*' (p. 38)) and briefly named in *Party Frock*.

WWII Timeline

Events:

- **March 1938** — German troops enter Austria
- **1938** — Gas masks issued
- **1-3 Sept** — Evacuation
- **Phoney war** — 3 Sep 1939 – 10 May 1940
- **3 Sept** — Britain declares war on Germany
- **26 May – 4 Jun** — Dunkirk evacuation
- **Battle of Britain** — 10 Jul 1940 – 31 Oct 1940
- **22 Jun** — France surrenders
- **Blitz** — 7 Sep 1940 – 11 May 1941
- **7 December** — Attack on Pearl Harbor
- **6 June** — D-Day
- **V-1 bombing of London** — 13 Jun 1944 – Sep 1944
- **7 May** — German surrender, VE Day
- **15 August** — Japanese surrender, VJ Day

Timeline years: 1939, 1940, 1941, 1942, 1943, 1944, 1945

Books / Works:

- *The Children of Primrose Lane* (1941) — Late 1940s
- *Curtain Up* (1944) — Aug 1942 – Dec 1943
- *Party Frock* (1946) — Dec 1944 – Sep 1945
- *When the Siren Wailed* (1974) — Late 1938 – Summer 1941

However, there is a clear expectation that readers will already know about the events. Similarly, both **Curtain Up** and **Party Frock** have assumed knowledge of Japanese war camps. **Party Frock** incorporates both VE (Victory in Europe) Day and VJ (Victory in Japan – now more commonly known as Victory in the Pacific) Day. There is a sense throughout the book that the war is coming to an end. However, the focus is on the local impact, rather than what is actually happening in the world at large:

> The VE-Day celebrations had been so exciting that nobody could settle down ... They rushed about and lit bonfires, walked in the torchlight procession, took part in the sports and went to a dance given by the Americans at the camp. (p. 79)
>
> That night, at midnight, news came which stopped all work on the pageant for five days. The Japanese had capitulated. There was a public holiday for VJ Day. (p. 200)

This would probably have been a reminder to contemporary readers of how they, themselves, had experienced the end of the war. It also seems likely that these readers would have felt the significance of the fact that, early in the book, the children decide on that the pageant will be held on 20 September: they would have been very aware of the dates 15 August (Japanese surrender) and 2 September (the official end of the war).

By contrast, **When the Siren Wailed** contains careful descriptions of key events of the war. Sometimes this is by way of a character explaining things to the children, and sometimes from the narrator:

> 'Today,' he said, 'Germany has invaded Holland, Belgium and Luxembourg by both land and air. They have all appealed to us for help. Mr Chamberlain is no longer our Prime Minister. We have now a new name to remember. It is Mr Winston Churchill. Now say that name after me.' (p. 45)
>
> The previous Christmas the Japanese had bombed a place called Pearl Harbor [which] had the effect, so they learned, of bringing the Americans into the war. This, they were told, was because the Japanese were allies of the Germans, so the Americans too were enemies of the Germans. (p. 150)

As a young reader in the 1970s, this book was my first exposure to the Dunkirk evacuation, and I found the description very evocative:

> 'Today,' the Colonel said, 'is a day we shall remember all our lives. Our army is cut off here.' He laid his hand on the piece of France marked Dunkirk. 'There were far too many men for our naval ships to carry so everybody who had even a little rowing boat was asked to help. And they came. All the tugs from the Thames – you children will have seen those – pleasure steamers, motor boats, drifters, tramps, trawlers – anything that could float. Mr Churchill told the House of Commons that he feared that only about twenty to thirty thousand men could be rescued, instead over 335,000 men, French and British, are now safe on this island.' (pp. 45-46)

However, there are still occasions where events are mentioned rather than explained in detail:

> The war was scarcely mentioned in front of the children. At school they were told about the sinking of the P&O liner Rawalpindi, to show how brave British sailors were. After being told the story they all sang 'Eternal Father strong to save' followed by 'God save the King'. This made a pleasant change in school routine so the children wished it could happen more often. It did not, however, bring the war nearer for few of the children had seen the sea let alone a big ship. (p 43)

We can't know whether Streatfeild forgot that this reference might not be meaningful to her readers, or if she felt that in this instance, the detail was less important than the mood.

Evacuation

The Government Evacuation Scheme was a plan to relocate civilians, particularly children, from cities at risk of aerial bombing into areas thought to be safer. It was developed in 1938, began being publicised in summer 1939, and was put into action on 1 September 1939: evacuees were taken from the cities and billeted with families living in rural areas. As the Phoney War progressed, people who were unhappy in their new locations began to drift back to the city; but there were further waves of official and unofficial evacuation when the Battle of Britain, and especially the Blitz, began.

Primrose Lane, **Curtain Up** and **Party Frock** all assume that readers will understand the term 'evacuation'. Primrose Lane is in a part of London that is *'not an evacuation area … and not a reception area'* (p. 8), in **Curtain Up** we are told that children are returning to London to attend the Academy, and in **Party Frock** that *'Every woman in the audience had looked after evacuees'* (p. 250).

In *When the Siren Wailed*, on the other hand, we see the evacuation through the perspective of the evacuees, both the preparations:

> There was going to be a war and while it lasted, which probably wouldn't be long, all children in danger areas like London were to be sent to the country. Then rehearsals started. The children had to come to school each with a suitcase, pillowcase or carrier bag. In it there was only to be what each child could carry. (p. 13)

and the evacuation day itself. This is supplemented with an authorial description of the operation as a whole:

> Though, of course, they did not know this, the evacuation named 'Operation Pied Piper' had been planned for at least a year and worked on ever since. On that Friday and during the next two days 827,000 schoolchildren were evacuated to so-called 'safe areas' all over the country. (p. 15)

The book also presents – through a combination of children's perspective and narration – some of the issues that arose with city children fitting in with foster families in the country.

Unlike in the contemporary books, evacuation is a key element of the plot in *When the Siren Wailed*, and there is a deliberate attempt to explain it, and make it real, for readers who were completely unfamiliar with it.

Gas Masks

Gas had been used a great deal on the front lines during World War I, and in the lead up to World War II there was a fear that it might be used against civilian populations. In 1938, the British government arranged for the production and distribution of gas masks to every member of the public.

The issuing of gas masks is a key part of the opening chapter in *When the Siren Wailed*:

> The masks were made of black india-rubber with a sticking-out round metal nose. For little children like Tim, who was only four at the time, there was another sort of mask made like Micky Mouse. Laura thought the Micky Mouse kind were worse than the black kind for Micky Mouse was meant to be a friendly character. Now, turned into a mask and clamped over the small children's faces, he became horrible. (p. 9)

This is accompanied by an illustration of a gas mask being fitted (although not one of the Micky Mouse kind – perhaps Disney refused permission).

After this point, gas masks are only mentioned once in the book: *'With our gas masks, we can't carry no more'* (p. 69). There is a similar lack of reference to gas masks in the other books: no mention at all in **Curtain Up**, one comment in **Primrose Lane** and a passing reference in **Party Frock**. This is probably a reflection of the fact that gas masks were not ever needed, and people gradually got out of the way of carrying them, particularly by the time the contemporary books were written and set. It is notable that gas masks don't appear in any of the contemporary books' illustrations – not even one in **Curtain Up** of a train carriage in 1942, where people were presumably carrying all their regular bits and pieces. While the opening chapter of **When the Siren Wailed** is set earlier in the war than any of the contemporary books, it seems likely that, even if one of those books had included the pre-war period, it would not have included such a detailed explanation.

Rationing
Food Rationing

At the time World War II began, the United Kingdom was importing a great deal of its food. One of the German strategies was to attack shipping, hoping to starve the nation. To deal with this, the Ministry of Food introduced a rationing system, where every person received a book of coupons. Rationed items could still be bought (although there were shortages) but as well as paying for them, purchasers needed to produce their ration books, and shopkeepers would cancel coupons for the items. Food rationing began in January 1940, with bacon, butter and sugar. There is no mention of it in **Primrose Lane**, although a description of items being bought for a party might have been designed to appeal to readers feeling the lack of nice food.

Food shortages are a part of daily life in **Curtain Up** and the need for coupons accepted without explanation:

The sight of real egg and chocolate biscuits both at the same minute excited the other passengers so much that in no time they were talking like old friends. Of course the conversation was mostly food, but food was what grown-up people liked talking about' (p. 20)

'I've got what's left of our week's rations in the box I'll give you afterwards. I'll just go to the Food Office about our change of address tomorrow' (p. 43)

Party Frock and **When the Siren Wailed** are set mostly or entirely in the country, where the impact of rationing was slightly reduced. However, we again see a contrast between passing references in *Party Frock* as against explanations in *When the Siren Wailed*: *'U-boats were sinking even larger numbers of ships and this meant food was growing scarcer every day'*. The practicalities of coupons are not mentioned in *When the Siren Wailed*, although it does contain the only reference to – and explanation of – the black market: *'The black market meant cheating the rest of the country by sneaking more than your share of what was rationed'* (p. 131).

Of course, for children one of the impacts of rationing was the lack of sweets, and this features in all of the post-1940 books – particularly with the excitement of food parcels from abroad, and American solders bringing chocolate and gum.

Clothes Rationing

Clothes rationing was introduced in June 1941, mainly because of the increasing need to produce uniforms. Clothing coupons were based on points, with an item's point value being based on the amount of material used, and also the amount of labour.

Clothes were very important to Noel Streatfeild. We see this particularly in books such as *Ballet Shoes* and *The Bell Family*, where lack of money makes it difficult to get the right clothes for the occasion. So it is not surprising that clothes rationing features significantly in several of her wartime books. *Primrose Lane* predates clothes rationing, but in *Curtain Up* the need for clothing coupons is an ongoing theme:

> They were so used to coupons, or rather lack of them, that they knew they could not have clothes just because they needed them. (p. 88)
> She had her school velvet, but it had been outgrown before Grandfather died, and she had been meant to have another as soon as the coupons would run to it. (p. 162)
> 'I don't believe we've got many coupons left, and I don't think Hannah will let me spend them on a real party frock.' (p. 177)

When the children start at the Children's Academy, they are given the same uniform list as the Fossils received in *Ballet Shoes*. But where the adults in *Ballet Shoes* are able to get everything assembled, in *Curtain Up* 'Hannah knew what state the children's coupon books were in, so she just stared at the list, looking hopeless' (p. 66). Fortunately for Hannah, there have been some modifications for wartime conditions. And some of the other clothing problems (including Sorrel's need for an opening night dress) are dealt with by using material from dresses bought before the war.

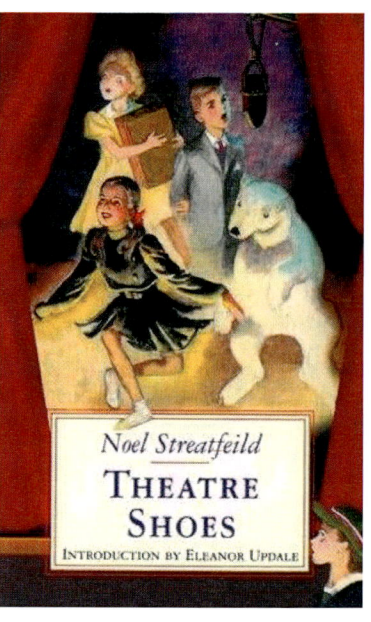

Implicitly, clothes rationing forms the whole basis of ***Party Frock***, as the general lack of new clothes adds to the excitement of an American parcel containing a party frock and shoes. It is also relevant when it comes to costuming for the pageant. Early in the book, the children's mother says *'There has been clothes rationing since 1941 ... There isn't sufficient material in this house going a-begging to make a pageant costume for a mouse'* (p. 31), and Chapter 14 is entirely about how this issue is solved (a combination of hired costumes, black out material, and, as in ***Curtain Up***, fabric from items bought before the war).

However, in neither book is the mechanics of rationing in any way described. In ***Curtain Up***, the need for coupons (both food and clothing) is as self-evident as the need for money; and in ***Party Frock***, statements such as *'Is there any material that isn't on coupons?'*, and references to black out material, are presented equally without explanation. Readers of the time had a complete understanding of the context, but for later generations it would prove rather more mysterious.

Interestingly, ***When the Siren Wailed***, written precisely for these later generations, also avoids detailed explanation of clothes rationing, as it did of food rationing. In fact, the issue only comes up once, with the concept being explicitly introduced (unlike in the contemporary works) but still not explained: *'All clothes were rationed so there was no one in the village who could spare anything'* (p. 152). However, it should be noted that while this story extends through to 1943, the vast majority of the events in it take place prior to the introduction of rationing.

Bombing

None of the contemporary books are written or set during the height of the Blitz or the V-1 bombing of London. As such, it is hardly surprising that none of them has more than a single, passing reference to air raids: the two books set in London mention them without explanation - *'we'll take cover if there's an air raid'* (***Primrose Lane***, p. 169), *'owing to the possibility of air-raids'* (***Curtain Up***, p. 101) – while the pageant in ***Party Frock*** includes someone dressed in an air-raid warden's suit, and the wailing of a siren.

As its title suggests, however, ***When the Siren Wailed*** does explicitly present the Blitz. While the children are in the country this is somewhat at a distance, but Noel Streatfeild structured her plot to have the children briefly returning to London in 1941, giving her the opportunity to present an explicit description of something she had experienced so many times herself: an air raid on the capital. The children spend the night in a Rest Centre, go to the basement when the bombing starts and are trapped there after a bomb hits. However, while details are given of the events, and we see that what is quite new to the children has become a matter-of-fact experience to Londoners, there is little attempt to capture the visceral experience of an air raid shelter.

In addition to public air raid shelters (frequently in existing tunnels, such as tube stations), the British government also provided individual shelters, such as Anderson shelters. These were distributed in 1939, with householders who earned less than £5 a week receiving them free of charge. Every family has one in *Primrose Lane*, but there is a clear assumption that the reader knows what they are:

> When war was declared the gardens in the Lane had to change, partly to make room for the Anderson shelters, and partly because the Smiths and the Browns and the Evanses, like every one else, were digging for victory. (pp. 6-7)

One family converts the garden entirely to vegetables, including marrows on the Anderson; the second grows cabbages, but replants their roses around the Anderson; and the third hangs a geranium in a basket at the Anderson entrance, and places a sign saying 'THUMBS UP' over the door. Non-contemporary readers can see from the description that an Anderson shelter is an outdoor structure, but would not necessarily be able to visualise it, and would need to deduce its purpose, as no information is given. None of the other books mention Anderson shelters, or any other type of individual shelter.

In both *Curtain Up* and *When the Siren Wailed*, the main characters arrive in bombed London, and are shocked by what they see, a moment illustrated in *When the Siren Wailed*. Both books offer a description of the bombed houses, and capture the emotions of the children. The following is from *Curtain Up*:

> Number 14 looked as if it was the only house in its bit of the square that was being lived in. Number 11 had been blown away by a bomb and nothing was left of it but different-coloured walls and some mantelpieces, which were part of the wall of Number 10, and some more wallpapers and a piece of staircase and a door, which were part of the wall of Number 12. The other houses within sight looked rather battered, and some had lost bits of themselves and it was clear no one lived in them, for they had large

E's painted on the doors. ... [The children] stood staring round with horror written all over their faces. (p. 24)
This is the only significant 'war description' in any of the contemporary books. Presumably Streatfeild did this because many of her readers, like the characters in this book, would not have experienced post-Blitz London.

Invasion and German Spies

The plot of *Primrose Lane* is structured around the capture of a German spy: *'If six English children aren't as good and better than one German man we might as well give up fighting the war'* (p. 98). But in spite of the fairly unrealistic plot, and jingoistic attitude, we do get a sense that children of the time were coached on how to deal with potential spies: *'Tell him nothing. Give him nothing. Try and keep him in conversation while one of us goes for a soldier, policeman or warden.'* (p. 36)

The other contemporary books, being more naturalistic, don't include German spies amongst their characters. However, *When the Siren Wailed* revisits the matter, carefully explaining a number of key aspects of home front defence: the Home Guard, Molotov Cocktails, the removal/changing of road signs. It even has a scene in which a German plane crashes, and the pilot is captured by an elderly woman and a young girl. But this is some distance from the lengthy pursuit of a spy detailed in *Primrose Lane*.

War as Background vs. War as Story

Looking at how these various aspects of World War II are depicted in the four books, we see some clear points that differentiate *When the Siren Wailed*. This is a book that tells the story of the war, incorporating as many key elements as possible (even if it did mean stretching the plot on occasion) and providing explanations for most of them. It recaptures the experience of children living in a time of great change, and presents it for a new generation. It seems to have a conscious desire to memorialise and valorise the British experience of the war, as seen, for example, in the description of the Dunkirk evacuation.

When I first began working on this presentation, I felt that these four books fell into two distinct categories: on the one hand, a historical work, chronicling the war; and on the other, the three contemporary works in which the war played a background role. But as I began to work through the books, I realised that *Party Frock* actually stands slightly apart from the other contemporary books.

Primrose Lane and *Curtain Up* are not set in times of great change – the war is a constant, and neither author nor readers know how long it will continue for, or what the outcome will be. Rationing is ever-present but not explained, and other elements are only mentioned in passing. In these books, Noel Streatfield is not writing for posterity. Even the descriptive passage of bombed London was probably not for the future, but for the large number of contemporary readers who would not have experienced this themselves.

But *Party Frock* incorporates two key incidents: the end of the war in Europe, followed by the end of the war in the Pacific. Like the other contemporary books, aspects such as rationing form part of the background. But more than this, it recreates, for readers who remember it, these momentous events, and also, through the idea of a historical pageant, gives them the opportunity to reflect on their place in history:

> You've seen enough history in this war to make a pageant on its own. Dunkirk, formin' of the Home Guard. Never thought to see a khaki overcoat behind every door in the village, did you? Then there were the road blocks. And the removin' of road signs, and all the rest of it. You've seen some history all right, old man, and you too, Phoebe. You'd be surprised if you could come back in a hundred years. You'd find your part all written in the history books. (p. 40)

Geoffrey Trease and "the Toughest Fight Ever": Passion versus Balance
Sally Dore

Many authors who wrote children's fiction during World War II ignored the war altogether, for understandable reasons. Others used the opportunity to exploit the dramatic possibilities of war, or even simply as an authentic background to contemporary stories with other points of focus. Later, the War proved very fruitful for authors looking for an exciting context for their historical fiction. I had realised that Noel Streatfeild was one of the few children's authors who wrote and published books during the Second World War that were set contemporaneously and actually featured the War in some shape or form, and then revisited it later in subsequent books, so much later, indeed decades after, that it really counted as historical fiction. I thought this was a really interesting phenomenon to explore, since one can compare what the same authors wrote about the same subject in two very different sets of circumstances. We are delighted the Harriet Jordan has looked at Noel Streatfeild's books for this conference. I asked on the internet discussion group Girlsown whether anyone could think of any other examples, and despite many other suggestions, there was only one author who actually fulfilled these criteria. It was an author I should have thought of myself, since he's a great favourite of mine – Geoffrey Trease.

Geoffrey Trease was in the Army during the War, serving in the Army Educational Corps in India. He continued for the most part to write children's historical fiction during his service, following on from his first really popular title, *Cue for Treason*, published in 1939. But he did write contemporary titles that featured the war. Before I talk more about these, I do just want to mention two little paperback rarities published in 1939. *North Sea Spy* mentions the Spanish Civil War in such a way as to invite sympathy for the Republican side, and has a warning about the Nazis, but is a quite light-hearted spy thriller, an easy read. In *The Life Story of Marshal Voroshilov*, about the Soviet general and Minister of Defence, Trease is writing a children's biography of a man who is in charge, he says, of one of the two or three decisive factors in any coming international conflict, ie the Red Army, and *"He is also the man who, if he survives Stalin, seems most likely to succeed to his position as political leader. A man, in short, who… has as much present and future importance to humanity as any other individual alive"*. The fact that I doubt many of us here are now aware of him is due to his having been purged by Stalin.

In terms of writing set in World War II itself, there isn't an extensive number of books by Trease to compare, two written during the war and two written much later; but when I reread them all at once, the two pairs were indeed very interestingly contrasted. They differ from Noel Streatfeild's stories featuring the War in that they are all set abroad, or at least, I should say, outside of the mainland UK. The two written during the War were one short novel published in 1941 in a very floppy little paperback pamphlet format in a series called Key Books by Fore Publications, entitled variously *Undercover Army* (on the cover) or *Army Without Banners* (on the title page and in the running headings), and *Black Night, Red Morning*, published by Basil Blackwell in 1944. Both of these are set in the occupied Soviet Union and feature, as you might guess from the title of the first, guerrilla groups fighting behind enemy lines. The two written later are *Tomorrow is a Stranger*, set in occupied Guernsey, and published by Heinemann in 1987, and *The Arpino Assignment*, whose protagonist is engaged in SOE operations in Italy, published by Walker Books in 1988.

Taking the wartime pair first, **Undercover Army** concerns Boris, a youth of sixteen who is trapped on the wrong side of the river when the Nazis sweep into his Soviet town. He is rescued by a Jewish doctor and his daughter Sonia, who take him to the datcha where they have been holidaying, in the middle of a marsh. There too comes an old friend of the doctor's, a wounded Red Army colonel, and gradually an eclectic assortment of mainly men assembles in the safety of the marshes. Interestingly, the term that's used for these groups in 1941 is not what we might think of, resistance or partisans, but "guerrillas" – '"*Guerillas?*" *grunted one, raising his black brows. "We seem to be,"* Boris answered with a sheepish smile.'" At

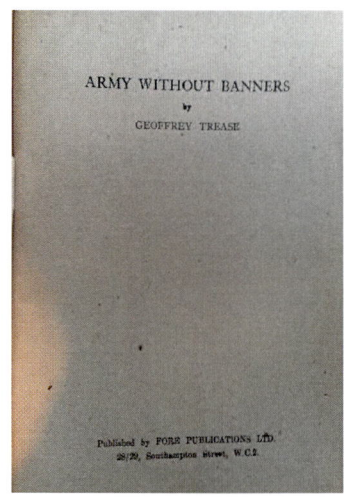

first their actions are on a small scale, burning crops harvested by the Germans, sniping at lorries, cutting telegraph wires and so on. *'"But it all helps," said Kamarev [the colonel]. "Suppose there are a hundred – suppose there are a thousand bands like ours, troubling the rear, an army without banners, but no less terrible? Think what it means – even in nervous strain! Think of the extra sentries, the broken sleep!"'* Then as they acquire more equipment, they move on to bigger targets, a column of tanks, raiding a food supply train, rescuing townspeople taken hostage by the Nazis in retaliation. Finally, Boris is tasked with delivering some seized papers containing vital information to Red Army quarters on the other side of the front, which he does in the guise of a

mentally deficient yokel, and then, refusing the offer of staying with the regular army, he gets parachuted back to his band – '*A guerrilla was reporting to local headquarters.*'

Black Night, Red Morning has as protagonist an adult journalist, Klim Alexeivitch Chernyshevsky – we don't know how old, but experienced and well-travelled, one would guess at least late 20s, so in this it's unlike most of his books aimed at children or teenagers which have main characters of the same age. In fact, the thing it most reminded me of was a John Buchan Hannay novel. However, I'm sure that the intended market was indeed teenagers, rather than adults (he had written some novels aimed at adults in the recent past) because it was published by Blackwell's in their *Tales of Two Worlds* series, which also included other books by Trease which are definitely intended for younger readers, *The Grey Adventurer, In the Land of the Mogul* and *Cue for Treason*, and it had blurbs for all three on the dustwrapper.

Klim the journalist, covering the attack by Red soldiers to retake a Nazi occupied town in spring 1942, is asked by a dying boy to take a message to a Moscow scientific institute in his stead, saying that Dr Victorov has succeeded in his experiments. He doesn't take it very seriously as there is so little information to go on, but back in Moscow, his friend Willi Schapper, an Austrian anti-fascist who's been involved in struggles throughout Europe (and who has a somewhat unlikely penchant for quoting Shakespeare), thinks it's something that should be pursued, and, by working backwards from the name of the scientist and an old report of what he was working on, the authorities realise that he has discovered a method of making synthetic rubber on an industrial scale that would be immensely useful to the Russians – and equally useful to the Nazis. So Klim and Willi agree to go undercover to Kiev to search for Dr Victorov, and any notes and associates that he might have had, both to preserve them for Russia and to keep them from falling into German hands. They create complete false identities of German businessmen, with forged papers and authentic German clothes, and are parachuted in. Various adventures ensue since Klim falls into the hands of the Nazis, is interrogated by SS Leader Otto Wolf and is about to be hanged before Willi rescues him with the aid of the Kiev City Soviet, an entire underground (literally) city of guerrillas hidden under the streets of Kiev. They proceed to track down Vera Kashin, Victorov's only surviving colleague, and then have to rescue her from a train taking enforced labourers to Germany, before bearding Wolf at his Crimean headquarters to regain the

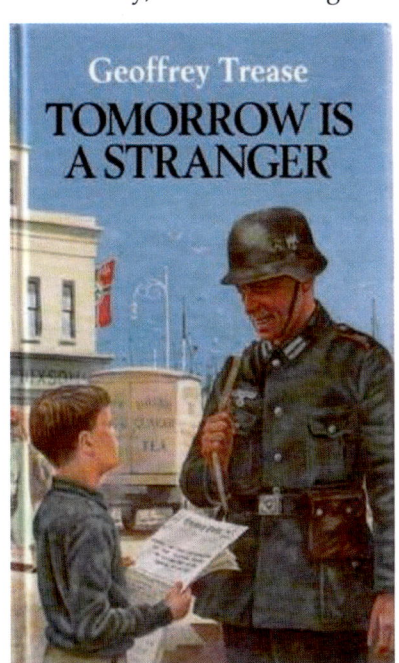

scientific papers they also need. It ends as they are being transported back to Moscow: '*And so... we passed from the black night of Nazi barbarism into the red morning of life and hope.*'

Tomorrow is a Stranger starts in June 1940. Paul and Tessa, who are in the same top junior school class, are among the Guernsey families who remain behind when the Germans occupy the islands. The book follows them through the next four years under German rule, living with the strain of the increasingly stern Nazi hold and the lack of food and other necessities, as well as the subtle means by which the Guernsey people undermine the German efforts while outwardly conforming. When the creators of an underground newspaper circulated clandestinely to provide news in the face of a radio blackout are arrested, Paul and Tessa decide to replace it using school typewriters.

The Arpino Assignment, like **Black Night, Red Morning**, is a little out of Trease's norm in having an adult protagonist as well, albeit one who is only nineteen at the beginning. Private Rick Weston is tracked down by the Special Operations Executive in 1943. They have been following up leads to find people familiar with particular areas of Europe where they are conducting operations. Pre-war visits to Rick's Italian mother's family have made him familiar with the Sant' Arpino area of Italy not far from the Adriatic coast, where the SOE want to establish contact with any local resistance. Rick, now a lieutenant, together with an experienced major and a radio operator, is fitted out with authentic Italian documents and complete kit, before being parachuted in to the Italian coast. At first all goes well, and they establish contact with the local partisan leader, but the major is captured, so Rick finds himself the acting head of the tiny mission, in daily contact through the vital radio with England.

The overthrow of Mussolini produces great rejoicing among many Italians, but any hope of a quick end to the war is quickly dispelled as the Nazis sweep into Italy to take over, and a much stricter regime is instituted. As the Allies invade southern Italy, it becomes clear that it is worth Britain investing in the partisans, and drops of weapons and other wherewithal are successfully arranged. Rick has been helped throughout his mission by a local family whom he knows from his holidays, and particularly by Lina, their teenage daughter who works in the local inn, and when she is captured, the partisans, with Rick, are able to rescue her from local German headquarters (to stop her giving away any information) as well as seizing important documents. A short chapter that is almost a postscript adds that after the long and hard winter when lines were entrenched, the allied push is about to liberate Sant' Arpino from the Germans, so 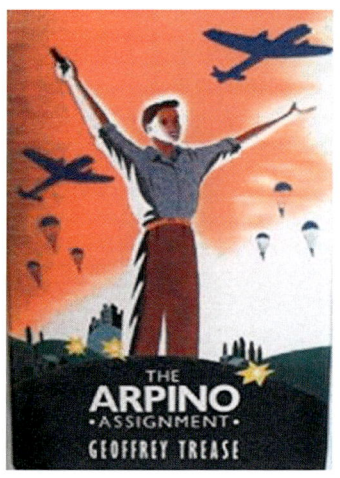 Rick has to move on behind the lines with the partisan group, but with that familiar Trease hint of romance, promises Lina that he will return.

So how do these books compare with each other? On the face of it, there might not seem to be much difference – all are set in theatres of war, and have protagonists who in some way or other are actively involved in resistance to Nazi occupation. Each pair includes one with a main character who is older than the usual age of Trease's heroes and heroines, so that he can write about active service more convincingly. And in each there are also feisty female supporting characters who participate in the action.

But in fact, the two pairs are hugely different both in tone and in the explicitness of their content, and reading them creates very contrasting impressions. The Soviet pair are vehemently anti-Nazi, reflecting in the words of the publishers' blurb *"the story of the toughest fight ever against the worst crooks the world has ever known"*. They vividly convey the sense that the war is indeed a fight for survival. They also contain some very heartfelt descriptions of the suffering of ordinary Russian people, and very graphic depictions of violence. Just to give a couple of examples, page two of **Black Night, Red Morning** contains a vivid scene of a boy of 12 dying, while one of many similar passages in **Undercover Army** concerns Boris on a raid:

A bullet flayed the boy's cheek. He rose on one knee and fired. The Nazi cried out in agony but he came on. The bayonet flashed, a streak of silver murder driving on through the dark. Boris yanked back the bolt, felt the empty cartridge spin lightly aside, thrust the bolt forward again, fired… This time the Nazi stopped dead, clapped his hands over his belly, and toppled slowly sideways. … Boris found himself on his feet, almost sobbing with exhaustion and relief.

Although the later pair contain scenes of suffering too, they are more muted, and really don't have the same visceral feeling. They are also far more balanced, with some attractive (or at least much less unattractive) Germans portrayed. In fact, I found that there had even been a German edition of **Tomorrow is a Stranger**.

So, why this great difference in the tone of the two pairs of books? I think there are two main reasons. The first is to do with the fact that Trease as a young man had been known as a left-wing writer, really quite radical in terms of writing for children in the interwar period, at least in many of his works, although he did also produce much more conventional pot-boiling stories to make his living. George Orwell described him in a review as "… *that creature we have long been needing, a 'light' left-wing writer, rebellious but human, a sort of P.G. Wodehouse after a course of Marx.*" His first full-length children's book, **Bows Against the Barons** in the early 1930s, was a retelling of the legend of Robin Hood and his men, depicted, as he later put it, as being more akin to a Soviet collective than to a mediaeval band of outlaws. As one might expect, it was translated into Russian, and was extremely popular,  earning Trease a large sum of roubles in royalties. The only problem was that he wasn't allowed to take the money out of the Soviet Union, so instead, he and his wife Marion spent six months in Russia in the mid-1930s, travelling around seeing the country and getting to know many Russians personally.

Trease was certainly not blind to Stalin's faults, but when the war came, left-wing feeling was particularly anti-Nazi and pro-Soviet. To most British people, the Soviet Union might have seemed remote, but it suffered very badly, more than any other combatant nation, with over twenty million dead by the end. I think these two wartime books were Trease's passionate attempt to bring the terrible Soviet experience more to the forefront of British minds, and in particular to create sympathy among young people.

The second reason I think these two pairs differ has to do with his evolution as a writer. I've mentioned that he looked back on **Bows Against the Barons** and thought it lacked subtlety. The pair of wartime stories certainly have a very clear message, no subtlety about them either. As he continued writing, Trease felt that sledgehammer writing was perhaps less effective than a more balanced approach, and in later stories, such as the second pair of World War II novels, he had fewer out and out villains and more realistically shaded characters. I think one can justifiably say that the later pair are actually better written than the contemporary pair, and certainly the characterisation is much more sophisticated.

In the end, I think it comes down to this. The first readers of Trease's contemporary World War II fiction, like Trease himself, didn't know the outcome. They have a sense of urgency, and passionate partisanship, due to the fact that they were part of Trease's personal war effort. The later works are very good stories, but however good a writer Trease was, it was perhaps inevitable that that sense of a desperate fight for survival couldn't be conveyed in quite as vivid a way when he was writing several decades later.

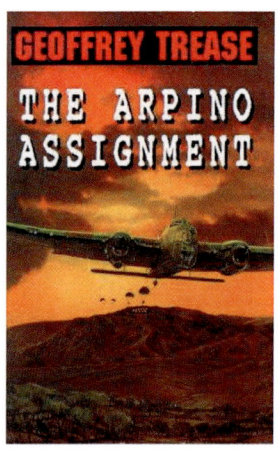

Bibliography
Bows Against the Barons; Lawrence and Wishart; 1933
Cue for Treason; Basil Blackwell; 1939
North Sea Spy; Fore Publications; 1939
The Life Story of Marshal Voroshilov; Pilot Press; 1939
Undercover Army / Army without Banners; Fore Publications; 1941
Black Night, Red Morning; Basil Blackwell; 1944
Tomorrow is a Stranger; Heinemann; 1987
The Arpino Assignment; Walker; 1988

The Twins Series by Lucy Fitch-Perkins and Others
Clarissa Cridland

I am very pleased to have been asked to speak about Lucy Fitch-Perkins' Twins series. I was read *The Belgian Twins* aged about five, and absolutely loved it. Later on, aged about 10-12, I borrowed copies from the library in Basingstoke. These were of course all the British editions, and I had no idea that the books had originally been published in America. Years later, on a business trip to America, I went into a second-hand bookshop in Boston, and saw a copy of an early American edition of one of the *Twins* books. It was one of those collectors' dreams, and I felt almost sick with excitement. I have a feeling I put the cost of the book on my expenses… (I wouldn't *of course* do that now….). I should say that almost none of the beautiful illustrations here are from my books. I am going to begin by talking about Lucy Fitch-Perkins, then I shall go through the series, and then I shall discuss the two First World War titles, *The Belgian Twins* and *The French Twins*.

Lucy Fitch-Perkins was born in 1875 and died in 1937. She was born in the last year of the American Civil War, and grew up in several Northern States which affected how she thought about things. Her publishers, Houghton Mifflin, were based in Boston – which was a very Puritan city – and again this affected how she and they thought.

She began with *The Dutch Twins* in 1911 – it had a beautiful dustwrapper. This was followed by *The Japanese Twins* (1912), *The Irish Twins* (1913), *The Eskimo Twins* (1914), *The Cave Twins* (1915), *The Mexican Twins* (1916), and then the two War books, *The Belgian Twins* (1917) and *The French Twins* (1918). In 1917 *The Dutch Twins Primer* was published for the schools market. It was a sequel to *The Dutch Twins* but it was not published for the trade until 1927 when it came out as *Kit and Kat, More Adventures of the Dutch Twins*. I don't have this one….

Then we have *The Spartan Twins* (1918) which was historically most inaccurate, *The Scotch Twins* (1919) and *The Italian Twins* (1920).

The Puritan Twins (1921) is a book about which I feel very uncomfortable. It is set in 1638 and features Goodman and Goodwife Pepperell, with their twins Dan and Nancy. The twins are given a black slave boy, Zeb. At one stage, Zeb is kidnapped by

Indians and it takes the grown-ups several days before they go into the forest to look for him (they are immediately aware that he has been kidnapped but they get the house in order first). Interestingly, **The Puritan Twins** was published in the UK, and I think I must have read it as a child, but I do not remember feeling uncomfortable at all.

Next come **The Swiss Twins** (1922) and **The Filipino Twins** (1923). Then we have three American titles – **The Colonial Twins of Virginia** (1924), **The American Twins of 1812** (1925) and **The American Twins of the Revolution** (1926). Interestingly one title which was not published was **The Twins of the American Civil War**. I feel sure that by the time she was writing these books, Lucy Fitch-Perkins must have realised that the ideals fought for in the Civil War had not been realised. I cannot think of another reason why that book was not written. I am lucky enough to own **The Colonial Twins of Virginia**. I absolutely love these wrappers – the picture with the title changed each time, but the rest remained the same. **The Pioneer Twins** followed in 1928.

Then we have **The Farm Twins** (1928). It was published not only in an ordinary edition but a school edition too. It must have been incredibly popular, but it was never published here. And perhaps this is the reason. The first page reads:

> One afternoon in June,
> Mrs Tilly went out into her yard
> to take the clothes off the line.
> She took down a shirt
> and a pair of socks.
> Then she took down a sheet and a skirt.
> She shook them out
> as she put them in the clothes basket.
> "Oh dear me," said Mrs Tilly
> "All our clothes are so big.
> They are all for big people.
> Mr Tilly is big. I am big.
> How I wish I had little clothes,
> for little people, on my line!"

Well, you will not be surprised to learn that the next morning, on her doorstep, in the clothes basket, hidden under some washing, are two twins – a boy and a girl. And here they are aged about one and a half, and a bit bigger. The whole book is written in this type of rhyme, and when I read it for the first time in February this year I felt slightly sick.

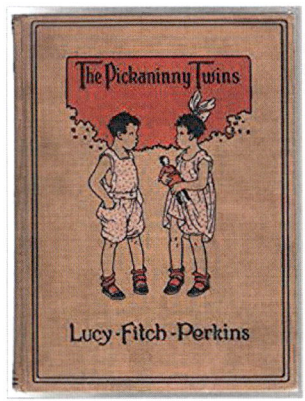

This was followed by ***The Indian Twins*** in 1930 and ***The Pickanniny Twins*** in 1931. I have to say that I have never read this, but the whole idea makes me feel very uncomfortable. But imagine my surprise in February when reading ***Enid Blyton Ninth Holiday Book*** published in 1954 to find a colour plate, captioned "The piccaninnies and their mammies are going for a paddle-boat ride up the river". I don't remember if I read this book as a child, but if so I certainly did not feel uncomfortable. Nonetheless, I should still like to own ***The Pickanniny Twins*** but alas, a copy is for sale on the internet for £100, which is rather too much.

Next come ***The Norwegian Twins*** (1933), ***The Spanish Twins*** (1934) and ***The Chinese Twins*** (1935). Her final book, ***The Dutch Twins and Little Brother*** was published posthumously in 1938 – I could only find a school edition cover, which shows that it must be very rare. I don't own a copy!

Jonathan Cape published the books in the UK. As far as I can work out, they published the first three in 1922 – ***The Cave Twins***, ***The Scotch Twins*** and ***The Irish Twins***. This was early on, as the firm was only founded after the First World War. From the early 1950s, Jonathan Cape published some extra *Twins* titles. I feel sure that this was because they wanted to tell children in the UK how children lived in the Commonwealth – and also because they wanted to sell more *Twins* books in the Commonwealth.

Daphne Rooke, who lived in South Africa, wrote three titles – ***The South African Twins*** (1953), ***The Australian Twins*** (1954) and ***The New Zealand Twins*** 1957). The first title was published as ***The Twins of South Africa*** by Houghton Mifflin in 1954. I haven't been able to find out whether they published any other titles. ***The Canadian Twins*** was published in 1956. I am not going to try to pronounce the author's name [Eva-Lis Wuorio] but she was born in Finland, moved to Canada when she was 13, and then later moved to the Channel Islands. ***The Twins of Ceylon*** (which I don't own) was published in 1957. I have not found out anything about Harry Williams.

The Turkish Twins which was published in 1957 is a really interesting title. It was originally written in Turkish and I suspect must have been published in Turkey. The translator, Dorothy Blatter, lived in Turkey and I suspect it was she who wrote to Jonathan Cape and suggested that they publish this title in their *Twins* series. Turkey was not a Commonwealth title and there would have been no reason otherwise to have included the country (it was one of only two non-Commonwealth titles commissioned by Jonathan Cape). The last three titles were ***The Twins of India*** (1959) and ***The Pakistani Twins*** (1960), both by Dennis Shaw and then ***The Twins of Lapland*** by Alan C. Jenkins. As this was a non-Commonwealth title I suspect Alan C. Jenkins must have offered it to Jonathan Cape.

All the Jonathan Cape titles, except for the very early ones, had an introduction by Rhoda Power. I absolutely love this, and always read it when I am reading a Jonathan Cape ***Twins*** book. It begins:

The small boy had been attending a christening, and the God-mother's promises, which some grown-up had explained to him, weighed heavily upon his mind. He felt that they put the God-child under an obligation – in nursery parlance – "to behave", otherwise the burden might be too much for the God-mother.
"Is it possible," he asked, "for a person to become a God-aunt?" I hesitated. "You see", he went on, hopefully, "a God-aunt could do all the things a God-mother does, without having to make awkward promises. I mean the presents and things. Now, if you or I were God-aunts--!"
I swallowed the bait and suggested that, as in his case there were certain difficulties, he had better leave it to me.

Now, I want to discuss the two War titles, **The Belgian Twins** (1917) and **The French Twins** (1918). As I said earlier, I was first read **The Belgian Twins** when I was about five and it made an enormous impression on me. My mother's copy was very similar to the one here, except that it was pink.

Jan and Marie are twins, 8 years old, living on a farm in Belgium. It's summer, harvest time; everything is peaceful and idyllic. There are rumours of a German army at the borders, but Belgium is neutral and surely she will be protected. The men of the village are called away to join the army. Then news comes that the Germans have crossed the eastern border and want to cross into France. That night their mother fastens a locket around Marie's neck, and tells her,

You must wear it always... and remember that your mother's name is Leonie Van Hove, and your father's name is Georges Van Hove. If by any chance — which God forbid — we should become separated from one another, keep the locket on your neck, and our names in your memory until we meet again; for if such a thing should happen, do not doubt that I should find you, though I had to swim the sea to do it!

(That is *very* prophetic!) When the "*great tidal wave*" of "*a long gray line of soldiers on horseback*" approaches the village, their mother hides the twins and the dog in the vegetable cellar. When they venture out again, no one is in the village. The twins join a flood of refugees on the road to Antwerp and safety in Holland. They are taken in by an old woman, then a family on board a barge who take care of them and protect them from noticing too

much of what is happening (burning houses and villages) but they can't help seeing all the German soldiers. Just in time they escape the siege and bombing of Antwerp and reach Rotterdam. They cross to England and are taken to a large country house set aside for homeless Belgians. The next stage of their journey is by sea to New York to live with a childless Belgian couple who have offered to look after them. When the twins undress that night, their American 'mother' discovers the locket, and realises that the twins' real mother is her sister. Later, the Belgian mother writes to the American mother, a telegram is sent, and the twins share their lives with two sets of parents.

The French Twins' story begins in Rheims Cathedral, during WW1, probably when American soldiers were in France, but before they had entered the War. The bell began to ring – it was not the chiming of the time nor the calling people to prayer but warning them that the Germans were at their doors. The cathedral is turned into a hospital and one day, the twins find their father there. Later when the city is shelled, they rescue him. The family leave Rheims and go down-river to their grandparents' village. Just before they get there they find the 'foreign legion' of Americans, dressed in French uniforms. Only 27 people are left in grandparents' village, everyone else has been driven away by Germans. An American truck arrives, American women come to help reconstruct the village. While the reconstruction is going on, the children manage to overhear two spies and report them to the soldiers. They are rewarded by becoming part of the Legion.

As a child, I had no problem with the Belgian twins going to the States – I did find it an *extraordinary* coincidence that the two mothers should be sisters – but I really did have a problem with the French twins finding American soldiers. After all, our troops had been fighting in the trenches since August 1914.

Of course then I didn't realise that the author was American and that the books had originally been published in America. But I was really surprised when I experienced the same feelings in February this year. After all I do now *know*.

I found three pieces of merchandise on the internet (I do not own them, though I should love to). Doll dressing outfits for *The Belgian Twins*, *The Japanese Twins* and *The Dutch Twins*.

These are the various wrappers used by Jonathan Cape (apart for the very early editions for which I have never seen wrappers). The dark background, white diamond came first, then the white background, coloured diamond, and then this one with all the twins, which as a child I absolutely loved. The title only was changed. Some of the books too were published as Puffins. If you Google the *Twins* you will find that, apart from second-hand books, there are lots of copies in print today – some as e-books and some as printed books. Some of them have original wrappers, some adapted for today and some plain covers. So here below is my bookshelf – the early American editions, the early Jonathan Cape, later Jonathan Capes, and then the original Jonathan Capes, ending with my very poor **Canadian Twins**.

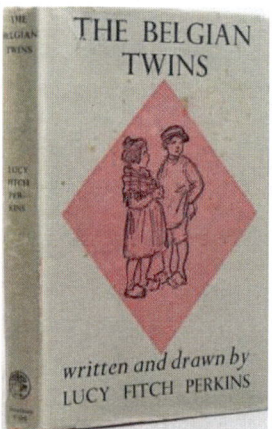

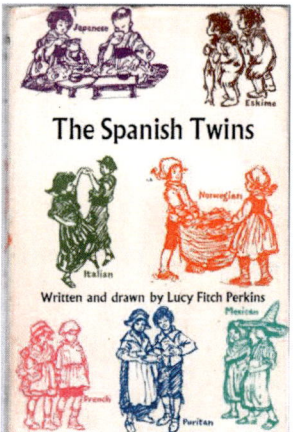

P.S. For Christmas 2018 I was given a first edition of **The Dutch Twins** (the first book in the series, published in 1911). Imagine my surprise, instead of finding the Houghton Mifflin edition, that this was a British edition, and not published by Jonathan Cape, but by Constable. The date on is 1912, not 1911, and so it must be an early reprint. The copyright date is given as 1911. What is interesting is that on the title page, is printed:

London / *Constable & Co. Limited* / *Boston and New York*/ *Houghton Mifflin Company* / *1912*
and the London is in bold, with Constable being *above* HM. Clearly what happened was that the sheets of the book (i.e. the inside pages) were all printed together, for both editions. However, it would appear that the sheets for the UK market were then shipped to the UK, and the book was bound in the UK. I say this because the front board is quite different to the American early editions, and on the spine is only 'Constable London' as opposed to having the names of both publishers, which the book would have done if the boards had been printed for both editions. If anyone knows any more about this, I would be very grateful to know.

Don't Mention the War!"
Ruth Allen

My talk looks at how "Girlsown" authors, especially Dorita Fairlie Bruce and Elsie Jeanette Oxenham, dealt with the Great War and its aftermath. My original thinking was to talk about the Armistice, and how it was portrayed by writers for girls at the time, and in the immediate post-Great War years. I remembered particularly the scene at the end of *The Senior Prefect* /*Dimsie Goes to School* where Dimsie's father hires a fleet of lorries to take the girls round Westover [Dover] to see the celebrations. But when I returned to the book, I found I was wrong on at least two counts. First, this was the commemoration of the Armistice, the first anniversary, not the end of the Great War itself; second, that although it had made such an impression on me, the mention is very short – a sentence about Daphne and Dimsie being away from school until after the Armistice holiday, the school service, and this announcement from
Daphne that forms penultimate sentence of the book: "...*my uncle has engaged some army lorries, and they're waiting outside. If we can be ready in two minutes he'll take us all round Westover to see the rejoicings...*"

I then tried to find other contemporary authors, asking on Facebook and Girlsown [internet mailing list] ... I couldn't seem to find any author who had dealt with the end of the War in itself. If any of you can give me any title of anything that is a contemporary account of the actual end of the war – in a GO type book, please see me later in the weekend! I don't know Angela Brazil's work well, so I have left her to Sarah Burn's tender mercies.

So I started looking at how authors showed the effects of the War, and indeed whether they mentioned it at all. You will not be surprised to learn that I have turned to Elsie Jeanette Oxenham, my favourite author, for my examples. This threw up some interesting contrasts, and what I also found intriguing is how as time went on, she – or was it her publishers? - chose to subtly alter the books to avoid mention of the war, or to distance the main characters from it.

Girls of the Hamlet Club was published in 1914, and naturally has no mention of war – it seems, on internal chronology, to be set from October 1912 to May 1913 in any case. In 1915 came *Finding Her Family* and *At School with the Roundheads*, neither of which have any war references either – unsurprising as they are likely to have been written during 1914. 1916 brought *The Tuckshop Girl*, also with no war references, and similarly 1917's *A School Camp Fire* has no clue that the War had been going on for more than 2 years. But *The School of Ups and Downs*, published in 1918, is very definitely set during the War, with references to rationing, troops at Victoria station, and Helen Robinson's fiancé having been wounded, but due to go back to the Front once they were married. In addition, the girls who were major characters in the previous year's *A School Camp Fire* come to Helen's wedding, and there is talk of the War work they are doing, as well as which services their husbands and fiancés are in.

A Go-Ahead Schoolgirl, published in 1919, talks of the War having gone on for 4 years, and the heroine's father is captain of a supply ship that is sunk by a submarine – as captain he did not leave when one of the lifeboats was found to be unusable. The influenza that was rife in 1918 is also mentioned within this title, as well as the information that Sheila Thorburn's husband of 2 months had been a Territorial, so went off to War in August 1914 and was killed soon afterwards. The boys in this title are also affected, as their headmaster's son is wounded, so that their school closes for the term, meaning they – after some days of mischief – are also set lessons by the mistresses of the school that takes over their home; although there is no mention of them joining the girls in class.

Ribbie's Book, published by the EJO Society in 1999, is a collection of letters between EJO and the little invalid boy mentioned as Wriggles in *A Go-Ahead Schoolgirl*. It seems that these were exchanged between late 1916 and 1919, and in these we hear of air raids in London, and learn that EJO's brother Hugo was in the Royal Flying Corps, and that EJO's sister's cat was called Sir Edward Grey and was exactly as described in *School of Ups and Downs*. Grey – from 1916 Viscount Grey of Fallodon – was a notable Liberal politician at the time, famous for saying, in 1914, 'The lamps are going out all over Europe...'

In 1920, as well as *The Abbey Girls*, which certainly doesn't mention the war, *The School Torment* came out. Here is another occasion of a girl going to a boy's school, something EJO has already treated in *At School with the Roundheads* (1915) but the reason in this case is that the school is short of staff because all the young men have been called up, so Tormy's sister is employed as a maths teacher. A Camp of German Prisoners-of War is also mentioned but the 'stodge' at the celebratory feast at the end is described without mention of rationing, although it is explicit that the boys would need a few days to get the feast together.

Twins of Castle Charming, also published in 1920, was almost certainly written earlier than the War; it includes travel across the Continent, and tells the back story of characters depicted in *Schoolgirls and Scouts* (1914). Similarly, the titles published in 1921 – *Girls of the Abbey School* and *Two Form Captains* – are free from war references.

In *The Abbey Girls Go Back to School* (*AGGB*) (1922) it starts getting interesting. The young men whom Joan and Cicely will marry are introduced to the girls at 'The Pixie's' class. The Pixie was Daisy Daking, and at Cecil Sharp House there is a record of her War service – as well as the diary of the summer of 1914 that has been published by the EJO Society – and various articles she wrote for the EFDS about that time. In *AGGB*, mention is made of the young men's military service, and Captain Raymond, who goes on to marry Joan, tells of the Pixie's visit:

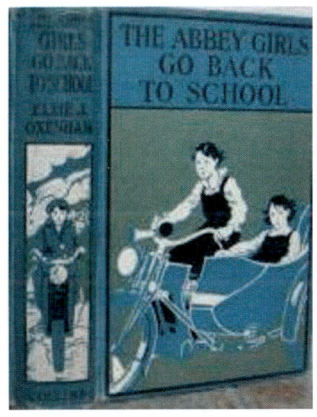

We were in a lonely camp behind the line...It was after the armistice, and the rest had gone forward to the Rhine. We felt as if we'd been forgotten by the rest of the world; something went wrong for a time and we got no letters and no news, and the boys got utterly fed up. So did we, and we didn't know what to do for them. Suddenly this Pixie...appeared in a car from a town some miles away where the YM [CA] had a hut. Someone had told her about us, and she had a few days free and came to see if the men would like classes. I doubted if they'd take to country dancing, as everybody did, but she was keen to try and the CO didn't mind, so she went out, speaking to every man she met, inviting them to come round in the evening; we'd found a small hall with a piano. A good bunch of them turned up and I went to see the fun. I tell you it was great! ... Next night there were dozens more of the boys! ... She was called away in a hurry after ten days, and the boys could have wept; I know they swore. I'm afraid I did myself. But they didn't forget their classes, and later we were moved

to the Rhine and found other girls teaching there and they were able to go ahead. They were awfully keen, and I decided if ever I got the chance I'd have a try at it myself...

In the omnibus reprint, ***The Abbey School***, published later in the 1920s, the wording is exactly the same, but when the new 'Fat Orange' edition of *AGGB* came out in 1938, the experience is at one remove: *My uncle's regiment were in a lonely camp behind the line...They felt as if they had been forgotten...Uncle John said he doubted if they'd take to country dancing...He said it was great!...When I heard about it all, I decided if I ever got a chance I'd have a try at it myself...* It doesn't have the same urgency, does it? Far less of a reason for the young men to come to the class if they haven't had personal experience of the Pixie teaching their own men.

The description of Dick Everett's whereabouts changes too – originally, Cicely says, "*Mr Everett's father owns the coffee plantation next to Daddy's in Ceylon. We know his family quite well, though I hadn't met him himself until this spring, because he was in France and then Egypt in the Air Force during the War...*" By the reprint this has morphed into "*...I hadn't met him himself until this spring, because he was abroad – in India, and then in Egypt, I think – with the Air Force.*" It would be interesting to know whether these changes were made because the publishers realised that reprinting with the same wording would make Jack Raymond and Dick Everett seem rather old for Joan and Cicely, who are about 20 and 22 at this point, if they had served in a war that had ended twenty years earlier, and they asked EJO to make the updates; or whether the publishers wanted to reprint, and EJO said 'not without a few tweaks or it will seem odd!' The new wording is also used in the 1949 Seagull edition of *AGGB*.

There are other instances of a similar force at work, whoever instigated it. At the beginning of ***The Abbey Girls Again*** (1924), Biddy is asked if Mary is a stepsister. In the first edition it has: "'*No, she's my whole sister. She's the eldest and I'm the youngest. We lost three boys in the war.*' Biddy said briefly". By the Fat Orange reprint (1937) this has become: "'*...The three boys in between are abroad,*' Biddy said". No longer 'briefly' as they aren't dead, so she doesn't need to put a brave face on it, though this makes a nonsense of later statements about the sisters being alone in the world. Later in the book, when Mary Dorothy is

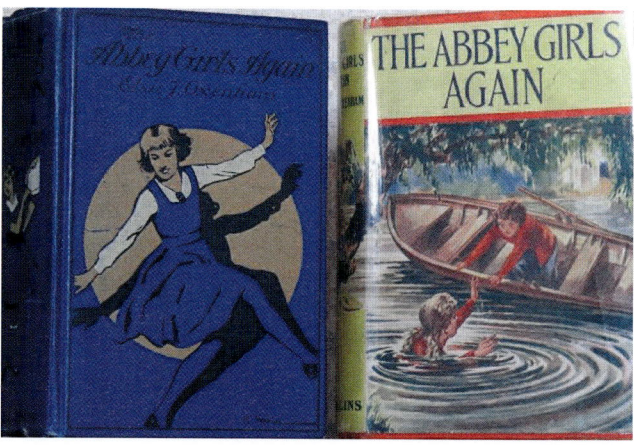

telling Joy and Jen about her father, in the original: *"I told you he was a journalist. It was the night before he left for the Front as special correspondent; of course only behind the lines – they weren't allowed to go everywhere. But he was to go where he could...He was taken ill out there and died before any of us could get to him."* In the Fat Orange edition this becomes: *"It was the night before he left for China as special correspondent...He was taken ill out there and died before he got proper medical skill."*

The next book in the series, **The Abbey Girls in Town** (1925), has similar distancing changes – in the first edition, when Ruth meets the Pixie for lunch and finds Andrew Marchwood already there talking to her, the Pixie says: *'I've known him for some time. I knew his young brother well, out in France...'* By the Fat Orange (1938), this is *'I know his young brother, too, incidentally.'*

In **Queen of the Abbey Girls** (1926) a similar rewording occurs – Nell Bell is telling Mary about her fiancé. In the first edition:

It was years and years ago. He was in the war, but he came through all right, and we'd made plans for our little house, down Richmond way, and he was going to be taken back at his job – a good job it was; we'd have been very comfortable. But before he could be demobbed he took pneumonia, and he was gone before I heard about it...

The Fat Orange of 1937 gives:

...He was with a good firm, and they sent him up to Manchester for a bit. Then he told me he was being promoted to head office and so we could get married; and we made all our plans for our little house, in Richmond. But before he left Manchester he took pneumonia, and he was gone before I could get to him...

Just as sad of course, for Nell's lost hopes, but no mention of war.' Later in the same book, the Pixie is consulted by Jen about her 'two men'; in the first edition: *'Her sympathies were strongly with Kenneth Marchwood, whom she had known during the War, but had not seen for some years...'* In the Fat Orange, this has become: *'Her sympathies were strongly with Kenneth Marchwood, whom she had known as a boy, but had not seen for some years...'*

By the time of **The Abbey Girls Win Through** (1928) and subsequent titles, the war was long enough ago not to merit any mention, hence no updating was required. It is perhaps worth mentioning that the Retrospective Abbey titles, which were published between 1938 and 1957, would, on internal chronology, have taken place between 1916 and 1919. Several anachronisms, such as transatlantic flights and talking pictures therefore appear far ahead of their actual invention or first occurrence, and of course no mention is made in them of the war which would have been going on.

But there is one tribute by EJO, in **Joy's New Adventure** (1935); when Maidlin and Gail 'disappear' to France they go to St Valéry-sur-Somme. There is talk of the effect the English soldiers had on the area, some of whom stayed after being at the nearby convalescent camp at Cayeux, and married Frenchwomen, running shops providing 'Thé. Like Mother makes it' in the interwar years. But Gail and Maidlin look at the estuary: *"It must be the mouth of the Somme,"* Maidlin said dreamily. *"The Somme, Abby Gail; where all those fine* *men died. I hardly remember it, and I'm sure you don't. It ought to be a sacred name, The Somme!"* In my timeline, Maidlin would have been 9 years old in 1916, so she would indeed 'hardly remember' the horrific battle, though it would no doubt have featured in the conversation of the adults around her, even far away in the depths of the Lake District, for no family escaped some loss from the conflict.

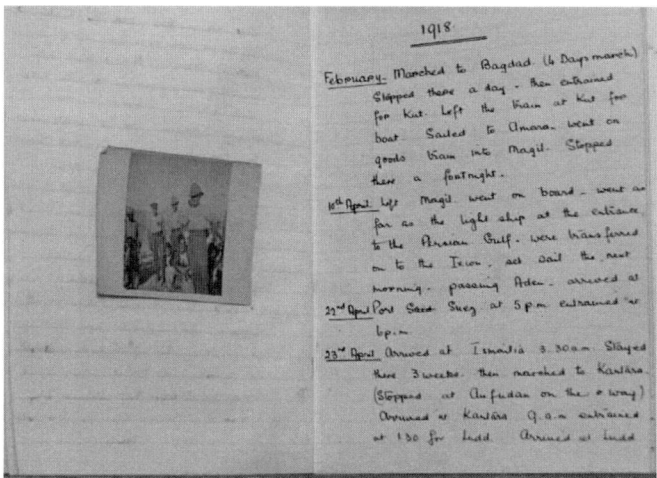

My grandfather was one of five boys. Two did not come back, and had he not had a slight wound, he would have been either on the Somme or at Gallipoli; in each place a brother died, and he quite possibly would not have come back either; my father would not have been born, and I wouldn't be here. I read my grandfather's war diary and am grateful for the sacrifices made by so many young men that allow us to be here today.

Angela Brazil's Wartime Books as Socio-historical Documents
Sarah Burn

Researching and writing this paper began from a sense that I ought to overcome my prejudices and read Angela Brazil's books, particularly those written during the First World War. I hadn't enjoyed them aged twelve or so, because they seemed to be set in very small schools, nor did she write series, and at that time I was under the spell of the Chalet School books, with their opportunities for character development and long, evolving narratives.

My recent interest in Brazil and her First World War books increased as I realised their value as sociological and historical texts, and I am delighted to have this opportunity to talk about them from this fascinating viewpoint. It involves reading her books with a forensic eye that notices and celebrates the differences between her experience and my experience. It necessitates having faith in the integrity of the author and believing that she is being honest with her readers. Identifying something that was obviously an everyday matter for Brazil and her readers, but which may be unknown today, or perhaps considered politically incorrect, also enables me to overlook deficiencies of style and plot. Her books can now be valued and appreciated for their historical authenticity and as a lens through which we may view aspects of society one hundred years ago. I am not going to mention the outdated stereotypical critical history of Angela Brazil and her books. Thankfully, it has been overturned by such writers as Rosemary Auchmuty, Judith Humphrey and Judy Simons. They convincingly explain the value of girls' school stories, the importance of female friendships and of how fictional creations, particularly those of Elinor Brent-Dyer and Elsie J. Oxenham, have become realities for so many of us.

Fiction meets fact in the case of Angela Brazil because of the mirroring of the historical situation of women in her books. The realities of women's lives during and after the First World War, the oppressive patriarchal society, and the rise of feminism, are all intertwined in her fiction for girls.

Elizabeth Bowen said of Angela Thirkell: '*If the social historian of the future does not refer to this writer's novels, he will not know his business,*' and this encapsulates my particular approach to Brazil's First World War books. Can this view of the value of a novelist's work in World War Two also apply to Angela Brazil's books for girls written during World War One?

An important element of the series factor that so attracted me when I first read girls' school stories is the ability of the school and its characters to develop through several volumes. The addictive quality of the series enables the reader to form a relationship with the characters, finding out more about their life and personality in each book. It is very attractive to authors for the same reason, and to publishers for economic reasons.

If child heroines grow up and leave childhood behind, the writer needs to be in sympathy with this and be capable of developing the child character into an adult. Angela Brazil did not write series of the accepted style, though some characters overlap in a small number of books, nor did she allow her characters to grow up. Judy Simons wrote in her chapter on Brazil in **Popular Children's Literature in Britain**, '*the majority of Brazil's novels, which, although they might pay lip-service to the idea of a life beyond the school grounds, essentially celebrate girlhood itself as a state to be enjoyed, rather than a necessary preparation for the life to come.*' In **The Encyclopaedia of Girls' School Stories**, the entry on Brazil ends,

What she revealed of her dreams concerned friends and schools ... They are a schoolgirl's dreams and it is no wonder that schoolgirls adored them and certain headmistresses came to denounce them. It also explains why Brazil's popularity among adult enthusiasts is *smaller than one might expect: in the end schoolgirls grow out of dreams and she supplied nothing to take their place.*

In her autobiography Brazil wrote that *'the schoolgirl's point of view is the attitude that has appealed to me most,'* and this is apparent in **The Head Girl of the Gables**:

There is very little more to tell. How Rosemary and Lorraine and Claudia prospered at their work in London; how Margaret Lindsay took a studio in town for the winter, and joined them at their hostel; how Morland went to the front, did a splendid unselfish deed, and won the D.C.M., are all beyond the limits of a school story, and in the borderland of the bigger world of grown-up life.

Reading Brazil's slightly unreliable and romanticised 1925 autobiography, **My Own Schooldays** and Gillian Freeman's 1976 biography, **The Schoolgirl Ethic**, illuminated the stories for me by connecting fictional incidents with Brazil's own life. Letters, manuscripts and publishing office materials relating to Brazil had been destroyed before Freeman could write her biography, so she has looked for Brazil within her books, which, as Brazil herself stated, contain people she knew and incidents and experiences from her own life. Freeman wrote in her biography of Brazil: '*Surprisingly, in a form as defined and repetitive as a 'school story', there are continuous conscious and subconscious references to the events and emotional conflicts of Angela's own life*' and '*The transposition of her life into her art is a recognizable substructure to all her books ... at its most revealingly Freudian in* **For the School Colours** *and* **A Patriotic Schoolgirl**, *and at its dullest in everything she wrote after 1935.'*

One of the most important reasons for using her books as historical evidence is their contemporaneity, for she generally set her stories of schoolgirls at the time she was writing them. In **The Head Girl of the Gables** the head girl talks about the time when women will go into parliament, thus reflecting the current mood, for Brazil sent the book to her publishers in October 1918, between the passing in February 1918 of The Representation of the People Act, which gave voting rights to some women, and the passing in November, 1918, of The Parliamentary Qualification of Women Act, which enabled women to stand as MPs. Brazil's continuous writing career, and her output of forty-six school stories and other books, is perhaps unique in that it encompassed both World War One and World War Two. Her first girls' book **A Terrible Tomboy** was published in 1904 and her last book, **The School on the Loch**, was published in 1946, the year before she died.

With reference to the Elizabeth Bowen quotation, any reader of Thirkell's addictive Barsetshire series understands that the author is concerned with a very restricted section of society, mainly of 'gentry', of landowners and aristocracy. Thirkell is an onlooker and aspirant and her authorial voice uncritically affirms the mores of her chosen social classes. Brazil's characters also belong to a boundaried social order, mostly to a comfortable middle class with aspirations, high educational values and a social conscience, reflecting Brazil's own background and outlook. Her books depict the first great modern revolution in Britain, when the old order, defined by birth, wealth, land ownership and gender, was changed for ever by the First World War and the fight for women's rights. This informs our understanding of what life was like then, for it is not only differences in transport and communications that contrast with life a century ago, but also the more subtle differences in social class and the status of women.

Before The Military Service Act of 1916 and universal male conscription in Britain, men volunteered for the forces. Women were expected to encourage their husbands and sons to enlist. In several of Brazil's books after 1916, when conscription was imposed, the seventeen year-old brothers of several of Brazil's schoolgirls expect to be called up for military service. The message conveyed by Brazil is that military service makes men of them, physically and morally, bringing resolution as well as muscles to weak characters such as Claudia's musician brother Morland in *The Head Girl at The Gables*. The universal sense of patriotism of those Great War years is evident in Brazil's books, although in *For the School Colours* it is almost counterbalanced by a particularly strong anti-German tone, which may, nevertheless, have accurately reflected the mood of the time. In this book Brazil created a most unpleasant and violent German villain, really a stereotypical parody. Because he was naturalised as British, he was not interned. That Brazil's publishers were not averse to playing the patriotism game is indicated by the design for the front of *A Patriotic Schoolgirl*, published in 1918 before the end of the Great War.

From Brazil's books we learn that girls in the Great War expected to answer their country's call and do useful work after they left school. For very many young women this liberation gave them an officially sanctioned sense of purpose, motivated by a desire to support their menfolk at the front and by the wider demands of patriotism. But patriotic duty and love collided when the girls and their families had to accept the death or injury of those they loved. In *The Head Girl at The Gables* the eponymous head girl, Lorraine Forrester, has two brothers in the army and a third training for the Air Force.

> She began in some measure to realize her mother's daily, hourly anxiety about these boys at the front, and to understand how behind all the happiness of her daily life stood a nightmare, with a spectral hand raised ever ready to fall on those three best beloved.

Lorraine's aunt received a telegram and
> tried to face what the short message from the War Office really conveyed. Only twelve words, but it meant the hope of a family trailed in the dust. Lindon, their treasured boy, had "gone west". Well, other mothers had given their dearest and best! She would offer him gladly, joyfully on the altar of Britain's glory! But her face seemed to grow suddenly shrunken.

Brazil used the phrase 'only twelve words' knowing that her readers would understand exactly what it meant, the telegram including 'Regret to inform you' and 'killed in action'. In *A Patriotic Schoolgirl*, Marjorie and Dona's brother was wounded at the front and sent home for an operation. Miss Jones, a mistress at their school, encouraged the girls, saying that her brother had been dangerously wounded last autumn but was now back in the trenches. '"Are they ever out of our thoughts?" said Miss Jones. 'I believe we all do the whole of our work with the trenches always in the background of our minds. Most of us at Brackenfield simply live for news from the front." Marjorie's friends sympathised with her anxiety, for one had a wounded brother and the other had lost a cousin.

A Patriotic Schoolgirl is one of a number of Brazil's Great War books that includes both an actual spy disguised as a schoolgirl, and suspicions that one of the mistresses might be spying for Germany. Marjorie said, 'How is it that most of our secrets appear in the Berlin papers? ... there must be a great many people – English too, all shame to them! – who are receiving money from Germany to betray their country.'

While they were at school Brazil's girls raised money in many imaginative ways in order to support injured and captured soldiers. Sometimes the money they raised went to the sending of food parcels to prisoners of war, an official enterprise that by the end of the First World War had resulted in some 9 million food parcels and 800,000 clothing parcels being despatched to British prisoners abroad. Wartime knitting, particularly knitting socks for soldiers, was an ongoing activity, in both fact and fiction, though sometimes the knitting interfered with other activities. In *The Luckiest Girl in the School*

Winona would have taken her half-knitted sock to cricket also, but Kirsty had sternly made a by-law prohibiting all knitting on the pitch since Ellinor Cooper, when supposed to be fielding, had surreptitiously taken her work from her pocket and missed the best catch of the afternoon, to her everlasting disgrace and the scorn of the indignant Games Captain.

In addition to serving with organisations such as the Women's Army Auxiliary Corps, the variety of war work that young women could do included nursing, particularly as less-qualified Voluntary Aid Detachment, or V.A.D., nurses in hospitals organised by the Red Cross; they could work in munitions factories or in the ancillary support systems of crèches, hostels and canteens, and they could work on the land, doing the work of agricultural labourers who were fighting at the front. When Brazil's schoolgirls visit these places it inspires their choice of the work that they can do and the war service they want to give. Her books contain many descriptions of the hospitals, the canteens, the hostels, the crèches for the children of munitions workers, and the towns built for Belgian workers. These communities accommodated some of the approximately 250,000 Belgian refugees who came to Britain during the Great War.

There are descriptions of life in the trenches from brothers, toned down for their sisters, of course, and of hospital routines, food changes due to the restrictions on sugar and the substitutes for wheat flour, the quantities and cooking of food in a hostel canteen, the duties of a V.A.D. nurse, how smallpox vaccinations were administered, how babies and toddlers were looked after in a crèche, and so much more. The modern reader marvels at the incredible organisation and sense of national unity that lay behind it all. Brazil's sister Amy was a nurse, her brother Walter was a doctor and Brazil herself worked in a crèche and was on the local Y.W.C.A. Committee in Coventry, and so learned much of what was going on in the war.

In several of her Great War books, Brazil's stories demonstrate the interconnectedness of her various themes, including educational changes, schoolgirls gardening for patriotic reasons, the opportunity for women to have careers, particularly out of doors, and colleges for women dedicated to horticulture and agriculture. These themes also occur in Elsie Oxenham's post-World War One books. Many of Brazil's girls want to join the Women's Land Army when they leave school, delighted that through their wartime extra duties they have found a way of life they love. Patriotic motives were to the fore, but it was also an opportunity for independence and perhaps to make a career. The fact of being able to wear trousers was also a great attraction for many!

In *A Harum-Scarum Schoolgirl*, Miss Todd, in whose brain ambitious projects of education for the production of the "super-girl" had been fermenting, announced the first of her radical changes. ... Pendlemere, which so far had concentrated entirely on the Senior Oxford Curriculum and accomplishments, was to add an agricultural side to its course. There was to be a lady teacher, fresh from the Birchgate Horticultural College, who would start poultry-keeping and bee-keeping on the latest scientific principles, and would plant the garden with crops of vegetables. She could have a few land workers to assist her, and the girls, in relays, could study her methods. ... Miss Todd saw Pendlemere a flourishing Garden Colony ... Her girls, trained in both the scientific and practical side of agriculture in addition to their ordinary curriculum, would be turned out equipped for all contingencies, either of emigration, or a better Britain.

This passage gives a vivid snapshot of ideas current at the time and contains several themes for exploration and research.

Although only schoolgirls, they could do some seasonal work of national importance on the land. Brazil writes about this in great detail in **The Madcap of the School** when volunteers were needed to gather the strawberry crop. It was organised by a Government bureau, which provided tents for sleeping and eating. The girls mixed with many different people, including gipsies and pickers from the London slums, as well as students, journalists, nurses and social workers, the 'ladies of education' who were the targeted volunteers. As one of Brazil's schoolgirls said,

There's plenty of pioneer work for women to do yet. They haven't half exploited the colonies. Once we show we're some good on the land, why shouldn't the Government start us in co-operative farms out in New Zealand or Australia? ... Imagine a farm all run by girls educated at our best secondary and public schools! It would be ideal.

Finally, I wanted to mention Brazil's books written during the Second World War because once again she situates her stories within the actual events of the times. Some of these books are as vivid and authentic in their details of life in wartime as her better-written First World War books. *Five Jolly Schoolgirls* describes the evacuation of a school just after the outbreak of war, from an area considered a danger zone because of the armaments factories. Part of *The New School at Scawdale* describes the atmosphere and activities before the declaration of war in Britain on 3 September, 1939. During the summer term in 1939

Aileen was vaguely aware that there were many rumours circulating of a forthcoming war. Air Raid shelters were being dug in parks and public places, everyone was supplied with a gas mask, and there was an A.R.P. rehearsal at school. Some people declared that there would be no war, while others had gloomy forebodings. Her father, whose firm was making armaments, gave a non-committal answer when questioned. Cyril, now eighteen, had gone to camp with the Territorials. Veronica and Nora had thrown up their occupations to join the Auxiliary Territorial Service. Douglas was in the Air Force. Yet people urged that these were only precautionary measures, that the horror of war simply could not happen.

Illustrated by Edward Irvine Halliday here in their evacuated quarters during the Second World War are the girls of Penrhos Girls' College at Chatsworth House.

In conclusion, to answer the question I posed earlier about the value of reading Brazil's wartime books as historical documents. Yes, I do think that they are a valuable source of information about the period, due to their contemporaneity. I also think their effectiveness in empowering girls and providing them with valuable feminine stereotypes should be acknowledged and celebrated.

Bibliography

Angela Brazil (published by Blackie & Son Ltd; publication dates vary: these dates are taken from Sims & Clare: *The Encyclopaedia of Girls' School Stories*)

The New Girl at St Chad's (1912)
A Pair of Schoolgirls (1912)
The Leader of the Lower School (1914)
The Youngest Girl in the Fifth (1914)
The Girls of St Cyprian's (1914)
The School by the Sea (1914)
For the Sake of the School (1915)
The Jolliest Term on Record (1915)
The Luckiest Girl in the Sea (1916)
The Madcap of the School (1917)
A Patriotic Schoolgirl (1918) (also reprinted 2013 by Read Books Ltd in 'WWI Centenary Series')
For the School Colours (1918)

A Harum-Scarum Schoolgirl (1919)
The Head Girl at the Gables (1919)
A Popular Schoolgirl (1920)
The School in the South (1922)
My Own Schooldays (1925) (autobiography)
The School on the Moor (1939)
The New School at Scawdale (1940)
Five Jolly Schoolgirls (1941)
Mystery of the Moated Grange (1942)
The Secret of the Border Castle (1943)
The School in the Forest (1944)
Three Terms at Uplands (1945)
The School on the Loch (1946)

Rosemary Auchmuty: *A World of Girls* (The Women's Press Ltd, 1992)
Mary Cadogan: *Mary Carries On: Reflections on Some Favourite Girls' Stories* (GGBP, 2008)
Mary Cadogan & Patricia Craig: *Women and Children First: The Fiction of Two World Wars* (Victor Gollancz Ltd, 1978)
Mary Cadogan & Patricia Craig: *You're a Brick, Angela!: The Girls' Story 1839-1985* (GGBP, 2003)
Angela Freeman: *The Schoolgirl Ethic: The Life and Works of Angela Brazil* (Allen Lane, 1976)
Judith Humphrey: *The English Girls' School Story: Subversion and Challenge in a Traditional, Conservative Literary Genre* (Academica Press, 2010)
Judy Simons: 'Angela Brazil and the Making of the Girls' School Story' in Julia Briggs, Dennis Butts & M.O. Grenby (eds.): *Popular Children's Literature in Britain* (Ashgate, 2010)
Sue Sims & Hilary Clare (eds.): *The Encyclopaedia of Girls' School Stories* (Ashgate, 2000)
David Stranack: *Schools at War: A Story of Education, Evacuation and Endurance in the Second World War* (Phillimore & Co Ltd, 2005)
Victor Watson: *Reading Series Fiction: From Arthur Ransome to Gene Kemp* (Routledge, 2000)
Sheena Wilkinson: *Friends in the Fourth: Girls' school and college friendships in twentieth century British fiction* (Bettany Press, 2007)

Feisty Girls in the Works of C. Bernard Rutley
Kay Whalley

Feisty: not a word that was ever used when I was young – or even heard of. Now it means independent, tough, abrasive, fiery or spirited. Always used to describe girls. Doesn't need to be applied to boys because they were all of those things naturally, weren't they? But girls weren't and couldn't be. Girls were gently or otherwise moulded into the correct type of womanhood that society expected. Witness *What Katy Did*, Jo March, Wendy who doesn't ever fight Captain Hook, Dinah and Lucy-Ann in Enid Blyton's *Adventure* series who whimper on the side lines, and Famous Five's all-purpose housewife, Anne, who spends a lot of her time dusting.

So where did we 1940s and 1950s readers look for feisty girls? Bessie Marchant books? Yes, but by then she was sadly dated. I hadn't then read Eileen Marsh's books (the Marise Duncan books she wrote as Dorothy Carter). And I never took to Worrals, who was far too much a pastiche, or do I mean a parody? of Biggles. Worrals was another Famous Five George/Georgina, always protesting she was just as good as a boy or man. C. Bernard Rutley's feisty girls knew they were better than men and went straight out there and proved it.

So I read C. Bernard Rutley. He was never one of the first-ranking writers like Enid Blyton, Elinor Brent-Dyer, W E Johns or Monica Edwards. But he was a good second-ranking writer, along the lines of Laurence Meynell, Nancy Martin and Constance M White.

Cecil Bernard Rutley was born on the 31st July, 1888, at West Court Farm, near Strood in Kent. He died on the 20th September, 1956, so 68 years old, not a great age for the number of articles, short stories and full-length books which he produced. His older sister was Cecily M. Rutley who was ahead of her time in writing her beautifully illustrated nature books like *The Green Meadow* and *By River and Stream* which were published by Warne and which would now be classed as ecology. I researched his life after contacting his son, John, and all my information can be found at Reading University, thanks to Pat Hanby who collated it all.

CBR was a tall (about 6'2") imposing man, whose photograph on the dust-wrapper of **The Peril of the Bush**, 1950, makes him look a rather dour individual, certainly not the sort of person to have written the daring adventure books that he produced which so frequently depict strong young women. But John said he was, in spite of this outward demeanour, a gentle person, not at all a macho overbearing Victorian type of male, but was very quiet and sensitive, never getting ruffled or worked up. He made a living by his writing through sheer hard work. John remembers him as always in his study writing, or going to Dorking Library, which must have had an extremely good reference section, or else very helpful Librarians because the background information in his books appears excellent and very wide-ranging. He wrote at least 50 books for girls and boys, educational and wildlife ones as well as stories, and over 100 short stories for Annuals from the 1920s on – *Jean of the Mounties*; *The Girl from Canada*; *Tomboy Diana*; *True*

Grit; *Red Isabeau* (the beggar maid who was voted in as Duchess because she killed the usurper); *Annette Wins Through*; as well as *How Jean Bobbed her Hair*.

The first C. Bernard Rutley book I read was **The Crimson Rust** (1946), and this set the criteria for his feisty girls, although, sadly, I realised by the age of 8 and three-quarters that I was just never going to make it. **The Crimson Rust** introduces Patricia Richmond with her gleaming Titian-coloured hair, a glowing complexion, blue eyes alight with expectancy and she's vital and lovely with her tall graceful figure. Gosh! No wonder her father looks at her with pleasure, which is a little bit worrying in today's world, but this sort of thing was never noticed in 1946. Father, Gilbert Richmond, is the celebrated criminologist and detective, and their sunny flat overlooks Regent's Park, so we know what sort of world they live in. Pat's soon-to-be chum, Suzanne de Brissac, enters on the third page. She is tall and slim, with curling dark hair, and large violet eyes set in a piquant, expressive face. And she dresses well, but that's obviously because she's French and will doubtless have neat fingers to twitch her clothes into shape.

And that's just CBR with his main characters. There's book after book with heroines like Jean Fraser in **The Treasure of the Hills** (1948): Jean – tall, fair, blue-eyed, lithe, shapely, quite the prettiest girl in Beaver Dam. Joy Curtiss, in **Pursued by the Swastika** (1944) is easy to look at with her tall slender figure which is, of course, beautifully proportioned, generous red lips, deep brown eyes, crown of rich chestnut-coloured hair and a good-looking and intelligent face to boot. Another gosh! And it's doubly good when they're twins as are Jill and Shirley Ross in **Secret of the Range** (1949). Tall with deep chestnut hair, brown eyes, rich brunette colouring, and straight-limbed (they obviously lapped up their spoonfuls of that awful Cod Liver Oil from the Food Office during and after World War II. Most of us either refused it, or kept it in our mouths like Dorry in **What Katy Did** until we could dodge round a corner and spit it out). And, as for Honor Lang, in CBR's **The Ring of Nenuphar** (1943) – she's wealthy, as well as being tall and slender with rich corn-coloured hair and dancing blue eyes with perfect physical lithe grace. She's a Pilot, a first-rate horsewoman, and won Olympic honours for diving (that would be at the 1936 Nazi Games, wouldn't it?). And she has a rich explorer father. So how could we ordinary lassies compete with all this? I couldn't, and I doubt whether many, if any, 1940s or 1950s British girls could, but, regardless of how fabulous all these girls looked, and how superior to us they were, we aspired to be them because they were feisty.

These glorious girls actually DID things. They didn't whimper on the side-lines. They shot villains. They explored untrodden deserts and rescued their fathers and anybody else who'd been kidnapped and subjugated. They righted wrongs and, rather nice for them, made themselves immense fortunes in the process. They triumphed over the Nazi menace, and made away with secrets under Nazi noses. They saved the formula for a medication that was going to obviate most of the ills in the world. They didn't get engaged or married at the end of the books, and didn't even make eyes or sigh at all the handsome young men who kept appearing. They were Feisty girls! Which is why I kept on reading C. Bernard Rutley.

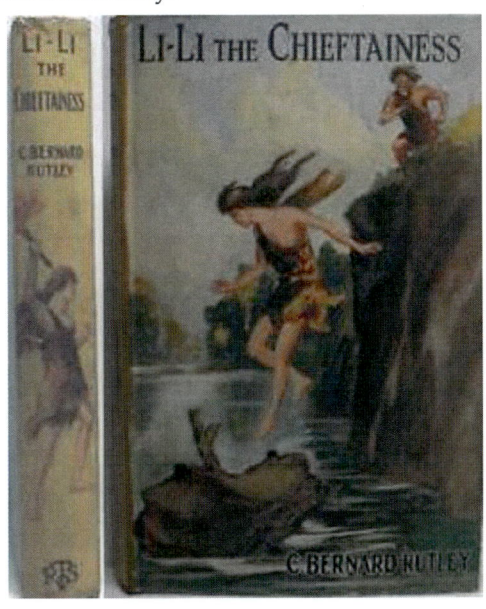

Even the earliest book I've got of his, *Li-Li, the Chieftainess* (1930), is majorly feminist. As witness the chapter headings: *How Li-Li became Chieftainess of the Fish-Eaters*; *How Li-Li fought the Swamp-Men*; *How Li-Li Captured Fire*; and *How Li-Li Built her Home*. All attired in a rather fetching off-the-shoulder animal skin cunningly covering all her bits, and always clutching bow and arrow ready to fight mammoths.

The Crimson Rust is where I came in. Suzanne de Brissac asks Gilbert Richmond to find her family's jewels which have been stolen by the Nazis. The de Brissac Chateau near the Pyrenees having been requisitioned by General Kurt von Ritter and his side-kick, Rodrigo Valverde, the day after the Americans landed in Southern France, von Ritter and Valverde left for Spain with the de Brissac jewels. They obviously hadn't got much faith in Hitler's strategy. If von Ritter was that fanatical a Nazi why wasn't he holding out until the last in Hitler's Berlin bunker?

You now need an Atlas for the next two chapters, or perhaps Google on your iPad. Pat, Suzanne and Papa fly from Croydon "Air-Drome" (don't you love these 1940s touches?) to Pamplona, where Papa drives to Jerez. They're frightened off by a threatening 7' tall Ramon, and also rock falls from above while driving back. Clutching pistols, they fly to Madrid, then to Lisbon then to Dakar – today that's the capital of Senegal, West Africa to those who, like me, are geographically challenged. They then need to fly to South America where most of the renegade Nazis are. But why are the 'planes all full when they want to cross the Atlantic? Pat vamps the Booking Clerk, and they're given seats on a Cargo 'plane along with two businessmen. Airline Security is non-existent which is a good thing as the two businessmen try to hi-jack the 'plane, and Suzanne shoots one of them. I didn't think you could shoot anybody in a 'plane because of cabin pressure, but I'm sure CBR knows best. They're now in Natal, that's Brazil not South Africa, and then fly to Bahia, then Rio de Janeiro then Buenos Aires. I've learnt more about geography from CBR's books than ever I learned at School.

Suzanne is related to the French Ambassador (I would expect nothing less), but why isn't he more excited about their story? Is there a sinister note in his voice? And when M. de Varenne whips them off to his isolated Rancho del Rosa farther down South in Argentina, I'm suspicious, and Pat and Suzanne should be as well. And I'm quite right, as Pat and Suzanne are kidnapped and flown (again!) over the Gran Chaco (don't close your iPads down just yet) to the North West Andes. A hidden valley containing - The City of the Beginning!

General von Ritter is a typical Prussian officer, tall, lean with a square head, thin tight lips and cold eyes. The City of the Beginning is a devilish Nazi plot whereby top scientists are kidnapped and set to discover a fungus which will kill off all field crops, so that the fiendish Nazis can hold a hungry world to ransom, and a New World Order will arise.

Fraulein Muller, hygiene expert and Doctor, oversees all the females. Suzanne thinks she appears quite decent apart from this kink about World Domination. Mornings start with a wash in bitterly cold water, then 30 minutes of rigorous exercises. Sounds just the sort of cardio work-out people pay for nowadays. A river flows through the valley, and Pat says they have crossed the summit of the watershed and are on the Western slopes of the Andes, so there must be a way out of the valley. I hope the geographers amongst you understand this. Exploring the native city they stop Rodrigo Valverde from hitting a child, thereby earning the gratitude of all the watching natives, and we know this will be important later. They meet Rita Carswell, here as a hostage for her scientist father, who fills them in on the formula her father's discovered, and the antidote as well. Always as well to have an antidote. So I hope it's both the formula and the antidote that's worked into the pattern of their undies. I'm baffled as to either how they've done this, or which undies they've used – vest, knickers or bra, and CBR obviously doesn't know either, as he gives no details as to how this is managed and, as a plot line, it's never mentioned again.

Pat and Suzanne try to escape via the underground river with the Inca natives who always leave the valley twice a year to collect wood and food. Sneering Valverde meets them at the other end (the cunning Nazis have always known about this exit) and they are brought back to The City of the Beginning and threatened with Shades of Grey which we'll go into later. Pat, of course, is a seasoned pilot, so they then steal one of the 'planes and fly out over the mountains. After a dog fight with the Nazi 'planes, they're shot down over Desolation River, and survive a blizzard, before being captured again by Valverde. He's persistent because The Cause is All. Friendly natives just happen to be there and stab Valverde to death at the last minute. Pat and Suzanne are now in rags demanding entrance to the British Embassy in Lima. They tell their story, and American and Canadian paratroopers bomb the Valley, round up the Nazis and free all the goodies. Grateful nations shower Pat and Suzanne with untold wealth, which is rather nice for them.

There are four Pat and Suzanne books: *The Crimson Rust* (1946); *The Mystery of the Everglades* (1947) which is pretty much island-hopping in Florida to avoid villains, although also taking in Barranquilla in Northern Colombia, not a place I'd ever heard of. *Outside the Law* (1951) which is a good story where smuggled mink coats, silk stockings, and boot-legged wine and cigarettes are distributed to the upmarket shops in Falmouth, Truro and Penzance. But Pat and Suzanne are made of good stuff, steal a Police Car and single-handedly (well, double-handedly, because there's two of them) put paid to the Black Market in Cornwall and the rest of Great Britain. And *At the Eleventh Hour* (1954) is where they're driving up and down France saving the life of Odette Martin's father (obviously at the eleventh hour!) and capturing villains alongside former Resistance fighters – all men, of course.

If four exciting books are too much for you, try the three featuring Honor Lang. We start with *The Ring of Nenuphar* (1943) where Honor searches the desert for her captive father, Anthony Lang, the famous explorer, and rescues him, of course. I don't think he should have got lost in the first place if he's a famous explorer, but there you are. *The Quest of Honor* (1945) follows, where Papa is asked by the Foreign Office to form an expedition into the Karakoram Mountains to rescue famous scientist, Andrew Coniston, who is being forced to manufacture Heelin, which isn't exactly the Elixir of Life, but it's better than Penicillin. Coniston would obviously give his discovery to the world, but he's being held captive by villains who want all the vast profits for themselves. So Honor moves in and shoots several people, all baddies, of course. And *The Queen of Lost City* (1948) is where Honor, Papa and Princess Zoe of Corinth (I'll tell you all about her some other time) ride horseback from Nanking into the Gobi Desert at the request of The White Tiger to retrieve priceless artefacts. And Honor shoots various bandits. But who is Natisha Sorensky? Friend or foe? Or fiend?

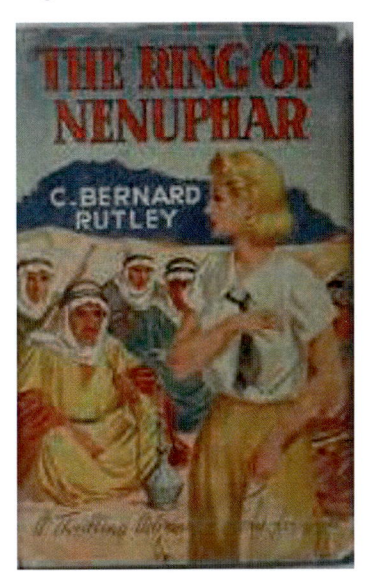

Pursued by the Swastika is obviously a Wartime book, 1944 in fact. Joy Curtiss is flying in from America to join the Wrens. She's sitting next to Suzanne, whose scientist father has given her the formula for Parroleum, a petrol substitute. The formula is now concealed in her suspender belt. This is surely the only mention of suspender belts in girls' literature until Valerie: Fashion Model in 1955. Nazis hi-jack the 'plane and Joy and Suzanne are transferred to a submarine in the middle of the ocean. Fortuitously, Joy has knitting needles and skeins of wool in her carry-on luggage, so she rather cleverly converts the Parroleum formula into Morse code, which she's learnt in the Girl Guides, and she then knits it into a pattern in a jumper. I can scan or photocopy pages 34 and 35 should anybody want to try knitting this pattern. It takes Joy all of 6 hours to do this, but nobody queries why she's sitting there knitting on a Nazi submarine when surely she should be pacing the cramped corridors and worrying about either being sunk by Allied shipping, or what's going to happen to her when they arrive in German occupied Europe. Das Boot this isn't! Suzanne re-sews the suspender belt, and they then eat the paper the formula is written on, which doesn't sound very nice at all. After several run-ins with the Nazis in France, hiding in tanks, and swimming across canals - because they're feisty girls, aren't they? - they make it back to London and triumphantly pass the formula to the 'right Government Department' as CBR says. We're never told which one. I think the jumper ended up with the WRVS where feisty older women unravelled plain, purl, garter stitch and moss stitch, and presented the deciphered formula to a grateful Government.

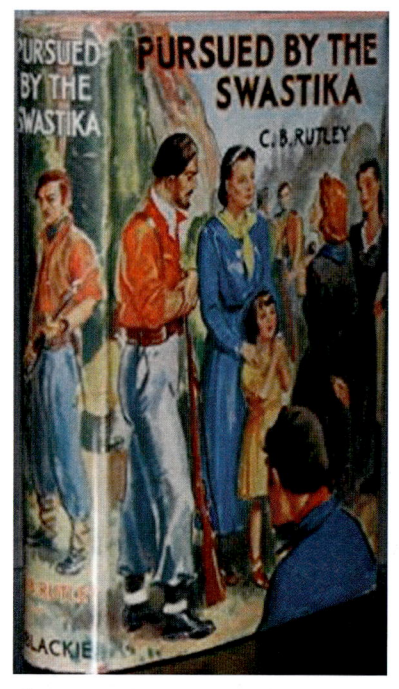

Now, according to John (CBR's son, remember?) this really happened. CBR's sister, Cecily Marianne Rutley, as well as being a writer, was a teacher, and a fluent German speaker, and, during the War, she worked at translating Prisoner of War letters, and, according to family lore, this knitting incident really happened, and I just wish we had the full details. It must have been a fascinating story. I still think the formula could have just been taken in to the British Embassy in Washington and put in the Diplomatic Bag, and flown back to the UK via Portugal, but then I'm just being picky!

You're getting *The Treasure of the Hills* (1948) because my older daughter, Elizabeth, lives in Vancouver, and her husband's brother goes hunting in Northern Canada once a year. Properly licensed, of course. In *Treasure of the Hills* Lorna Gray flies in from London to find and lay claim to the pitchblende deposits that her Uncle Stuart has left to her. And, fresh off the 'plane at Beaver Dam, the first person she speaks to is Jean Fraser (the prettiest woman there, remember?). The search for the pitchblende deposits entails living in a cabin near Great Bear Lake over the Canadian winter, which is pretty cold, I can tell you. I coped with 30 degrees below in Montreal and that was bad enough. How those early French emigrants coped I just do not know.

While Father takes the sledges and huskies to Fort Norman (that's called Tulita in today's world) to stock up with food and supplies, Jean and Lorna are out there cutting down trees and stripping branches for winter fuel which must have been pretty hard work, and packing moss into all outside cracks in the cabin walls. I'm so glad they're not doing a Doris Day/Calamity Jane and putting up gingham curtains and picking flowers and singing. Papa returns and, with some friendly Dogribs (they're either First Nations or possibly Inuits this far North), shoots 3 moose so as to have meat during the winter. Vegetarians, you may want to close your eyes at this point, because this is Bradley Haysom with the moose he shot. And that's the size of a Canadian moose. You can see why Papa and Big Bear will need very very well-sharpened Bowie knives, as cutting up just one moose Brad says takes almost a full day. Lorna and Jean continue doing feisty things like shooting baddies, and the pitchblende is claimed by Lorna who promptly gives half the profits to Jean and Papa, which is rather nice for them.

So reading these books allowed me to channel my inner tomboy which, living in a 1940s/1950s Birmingham suburb, had to be completely suppressed, until I could allow it free rein 50 years later.

I'll finish with the 50 Shades of Grey aspect. I refused to read *50 Shades of Grey* after some character offered another character cheese straight from the 'fridge! Can you imagine? Camembert or Brie straight from a 'fridge! It's just not on! But C. Bernard Rutley has an odd and somewhat worrying occasional fascination with communal bathing – girls only, that is; silk underwear; whips (think Indiana Jones) and girls' white backs. This is Tig Thomas' fault who first brought this to my attention. In **The Crimson Rust** Pat and Suzanne are threatened with being stripped and beaten – I'm leaving you all to read the details in the books as, as I said so often when working for my Doctors, anything below the neck I just don't want to know about. Reading this as a very young reader this just seemed another example of Nazi cruelty, but, re-reading the books today, CBR's descriptions come over almost as soft porn, and I just do not know how they got past any editor! Did no editor at Blackie or Newnes read any of these books? Communal bathing occurs in **The Crimson Rust** where Pat, Suzanne *and* Rita Carswell are in the bath together at one point which I would have thought was a bit crowded, and several times Pat sits on the edge of the bath while Suzanne bathes, then vice versa. But the most overt scenes are in **The Queen of Lost City** where Honor is forced to be Natisha's slave. Page 151 but I'm not going to carry on because I shall blush. But how on earth did these scenes get printed in girls' books of the 1940s and 1950s? I just do not know. So, if you can keep your eyes closed, and ignore certain pages, CBR's books on feisty girls are well worth reading for sturdy upright British girls who actually 'do' things, so hurrah for Cecil Bernard Rutley.

Writing About War - Authors' Experiences
Helen Barber, Katherine Bruce, Sheena Wilkinson

Among our conference participants were three authors who had each set books against a background of the First or Second World Wars. They talked about their experiences of writing, particularly of using war as a background in their stories.

Searching for Authenticity
Helen Barber

To date I have had five full-length school stories published, four of them based on or in Elinor Brent-Dyer's *Chalet School* series and published by Girls Gone By Publishers and all set in the early twentieth-century: one during the First World War, one during the Second World War and three in the inter-war era.

My research style for these books has varied greatly, depending partly on the depth of my prior knowledge and partly on what I was trying to achieve.

I grew up in the 1970s, when, relatively speaking, the Second World War was not long over. TV stations filled up their afternoon slots with 40s propaganda films—just the thing to watch if home ill from school; the BBC were churning out new episodes of *Dad's Army*, while friends and relatives still regularly discussed 'what they did in the war'. Added to that, there was a plethora of excellent children's literature written about or even during the war, including, of course, EBD's own atmospheric wartime books.

My first book, *A Chalet School Headmistress* is set in the same term as Elinor Brent-Dyer's *Mystery at The Chalet School*. This title slots into the *Chalet School* series within the wartime era, but, curiously enough, does not focus on the war. I decided to follow EBD's lead on this and so my research for *Headmistress* was limited. *Headmistress* was, in any case, a book which drew heavily on family stories and traditions. Its episodic plot is based on actual experiences, so when it came to adding wartime elements, I relied largely on anecdotal evidence and on the facts I had absorbed from all that ready-available post-war cultural material.

The Bettanys on the Home Front, my First World War prequel to the *Chalet School* series, is a very different kettle of fish. It was deliberately written to commemorate the First World War—about which I knew comparatively little—and so required a great deal of research. I read numerous text books, visited the Durham Light Infantry Museum (now sadly closed), trawled the internet and watched various documentaries, including the very moving *Last Voices of World War I*: a series of interviews with people who had experienced the war. I consulted novels and newspapers written during the period—resources that provide primary cultural information, without analysis based on hindsight—and importantly, I think, considered what EBD herself had written about the conflict, both in retrospect in the *Chalet School* series, and in her war poetry. I wanted to reflect and pay tribute to her attitudes and experiences in my own book.

When writing my two inter-War Chalet School prequels—*The Bettanys of Taverton High* and *Last Term at Taverton High*—my main priority was again to reflect EBD's own approach in this era. She began her *Chalet School* series not long after the First World War and is, of course, a wonderful exponent of the era's school story genre. Her books are lively, full of humour and positive—excellent comfort reading. Admittedly, they detail the lives of the privileged, perhaps assuming similar privilege amongst the readers; perhaps offering readers a chance to dream of a life they could never have. Nonetheless, EBD did not write in a bubble that is totally divorced from reality. She occasionally referenced the First World War and its socio-economic aftermath; she was sensitive about the issue. I have tried to replicate this in my books.

The setting for my final inter-War book, *Mollie's Choice* (published by Books To Treasure), is Durham City's Girls' County School in the early 1920s. Although the book's fundamentally optimistic plot fits into the school story genre, replicating my other books, my purpose in writing it was subtly different. I was describing life in a real school, in a real city and I wanted to get things right. So, once more, I did a lot of research: consulting books, trawling archives for topographic, historic and cultural details. Importantly, this book is not about a private school; its pupils are not from exactly the same social background as those you usually meet in school stories. Aware of this, I read up about culture and social mobility in the era. And, of course, I could not help but recognise the impact of the First World War on the period. Some novels written in the inter-war years—even feel-good books, like DL Sayers' Wimsey titles—do recognise the psychological after-effects of the war. I had already gleaned information from them. But now I researched the subject in more detail, learning more about the diverse mental health problems: the symptoms, the medical treatments, the help—or lack of help—provided by the state. And I very much hope that I have been able to convey some of my findings in my story.

Writing the Chalet Wartime Books
Katherine Bruce

Coming relatively late to the Chalet School – I was fifteen when I found my first title – I was already fascinated by the various challenges that existed during the Second World War. I had watched documentaries such as *The World at War* for years, and history lessons that focused on that era were far more interesting to me than the studies of ancient Rome or Persia that had generally been the focus of history at school. However I had always regretted that *The World at War* and other similar documentaries and books chose to focus on military actions and great leaders rather than the struggles and challenges faced by individuals. This was, of course, typical for the era: in the 1980s and earlier, little attention was paid to the experiences of ordinary people, and even less so to women unless they held roles of some significance.

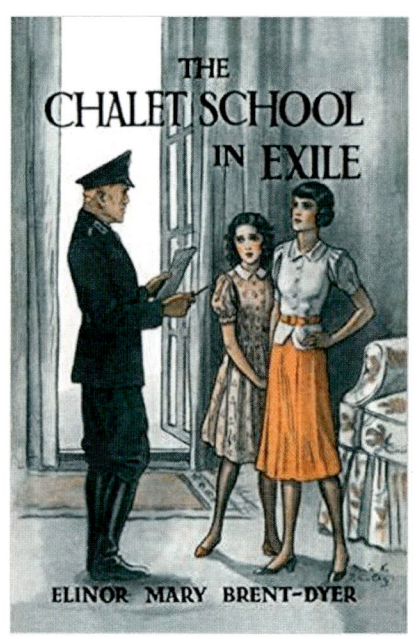

The Chalet School, therefore, allowed me a glimpse into the everyday world in which I had long had such an interest. Mentions of rationing, blackout, air raids, and other restrictions on people's lives during that time appeared in the very first war-time book I read – *The Chalet School at War*, as it was called. This made me determined to find the other books from that era. Fortunately my school library had a selection of Chalet books, including **Highland Twins at the Chalet School, Lavender Laughs in the Chalet School**, and **Gay Lambert at the Chalet School** (this being the Armada title). *The Chalet School in Exile* turned up at my local library. I was able to buy a copy of *Jo to the Rescue,* which had been published by Armada the previous year, although I was unsure if it actually counted as a 'war' book or not.

I was very confused about why this seemed to be all of the books relating to the war. *Three Go to the Chalet School* was clearly set afterwards, despite its mentions of anti-German sentiment. Later books continued to mention war-related matters, but it was clear, even before the first time I tried to sit down and work out a timeline for the series, that they were not set during the war itself.

While continuing to search for other titles in the series, I remained convinced that there had to be a book that covered the end of the war, at least in Europe. Ever the optimist, I even hoped to find mention of the defeat of Japan. It took almost five years for me to realise that I was looking for something that simply didn't exist.

The publication of *New Beginnings at the Chalet School* in 1999 inspired me to consider the possibility that I might be able to write something similar. But it took me another year or so to get up the courage to attempt to fill the gap I felt was most critical in the series. The first draft took six months to write.

That, it turned out, was the easy part.

Editing started as soon as the book had been accepted by Ann and Clarissa at GGBP, and with it came the revelation, common to all twenty-somethings, that it turns out I don't know nearly as much as I thought I did! Questions started immediately: what was the timeline I had established for this book and how did those books surrounding it fit? What about those long short-stories, *A Mystery for the Chalet School*, *Tom Tackles the Chalet School*, and *The Chalet School and Rosalie*? How could I explain some of the more peculiar form placements for some girls? Would certain events I had included in the first draft, such as mention of Marilyn Evans' term as head girl, or of Peggy Bettany's broken arm, really occur in this term or would it have to come later? Or earlier? And from a perspective of happenings in the outside world, how would the arrival of the end of the war have impacted the school? What took place on that day that should or must be included, and what needed to be removed? And how much of what was happening outside of England could or should be described?

Some elements of the story had to be removed immediately. It was not going to work for me to include the end of the war in the Pacific as this would occur in the middle of the summer holidays, not a period covered in any of the Chalet books. I could not include chapters showing events taking place in Australia in 1945 or include a romance for Margia Stevens. The major problem with the book as it stood in its original form, though, was that it focused too much on the adults and not enough on the school. Although Elinor Brent-Dyer is known for including scenes that focus on the grown-ups, a book which included more than half of the chapters with this perspective was certainly not typical. This was a challenge, though, because by including the mistresses and other adults connected to the school, it had been possible to explore political and social issues at a level to which girls would be unlikely to arrive. Removing much of this would take away a great deal of the glimpses into what was going on beyond the school gates – and yet, to keep the book within the boundaries of what was a typical Chalet school story, they had to be removed.

Thus a refocus was required, and it became necessary to choose new characters around whom the majority of the action would take place. This was one of the greatest challenges because each age-group provided the possibility of a different perspective on various events and activities that slowly made their way into the book. It was important to echo other elements of the *Chalet School* series that had played such a key role in war-time Chalet books: gardening, ordinary lessons, guides, and, as ever in Elinor Brent-Dyer's book, a key event to end the term. Of course, the announcement of the end of the war in Europe, and the school's associated celebrations, formed the crux of the story, although even those chapters changed as it became possible to include more and more details that were specific both to the date and the location in which the story was being told: radio reports, the music that was played, the weather, etc. But, of course, as such things were included, they prompted new questions. One of the most persistent that continued to arise through the entire editing process was the issue of how much people knew about the coming end of the war in Germany - thank goodness for the internet, which, after much hunting, allowed this and other questions to be answered in one form or another!

Over time I managed to rework some of my earlier, previously omitted elements so that they were suitable for inclusion. Of particular note was the information about Singapore and the experience of war in Australia. Naturally this is a subject that I find of particular interest, and, as with so much else in this book, it was a joy to have a reason to learn more about it so I could find the details I would include in *Peace*. The change in attitude towards history that has occurred over the past twenty years has meant that personal narratives covering this and a wide range of other subjects are now much more readily available than they were when I first began reading the *Chalet School*. Details from those biographies and diaries made their way into my book from the writings of other people – although I omitted some of the more gruesome details.

There were other items I included as I became more interested in different aspects of the war. The hints I supply of Amy Stevens being involved in S.O.E. reflect my own fascination with the undercover and spying work that was such a key part of the war, as well as being a field in which women could actively participate. Restrictions placed on guiding (for instance, the difficulties of camping and campfires, badges having to be altered slightly to fit in with wartime restrictions, etc) presented other challenges that came into the book rather late in the process, but which created questions and issues of their own. (The cover illustration was chosen a number of months before publication, but it helped to increase the role played by guiding in the story, although, of course, not without prompting yet more questions.)

Naturally there were other challenges in writing *Peace* than those I have mentioned here. Looking back over the emails and files I sent and received during the five years of the editing process, it must be admitted that much of the time was devoted to the issue of which girl was in what form or whether a particular phrase I had used was more Australian than English – a process that seems to prove challenging regardless of whether the fill-in is war-related or not. However when it came to the use of historical facts and questions, I was always determined to ensure that I had the details correct. As was frequently mentioned during the writing process, many of the things I was including had existed in the lives of some of those who would read the book when it was published, so I wanted to make sure I got them right. I must confess that I have never enjoyed making mistakes – the one error in the book continues to niggle at me even this much later and I look forward to a future publication of *Peace* in which I can finally correct it. But aside from my own personal considerations, in regard to key historic organisations or wartime bodies, there was also the sense that not doing the research somehow diminished the importance and respect due to those who had been involved with them in real life. This ability to respect and pay homage to those who went through so much during the Second World War was, and remains, one of the things of which I am proudest of in the writing of *Peace Comes to the Chalet School*.

Writing 1918
Sheena Wilkinson

My novel *Star by Star* (Little Island, 2017) is set during the last weeks of World War One in Ireland. I'm going to talk about how I came to write it, and the challenges of writing a book set in 1918, during one of the most turbulent few months of the twentieth or any other century. What with the Spanish Flu pandemic, the end of the war, and the intensification of the fight for Irish independence, there was plenty going on.

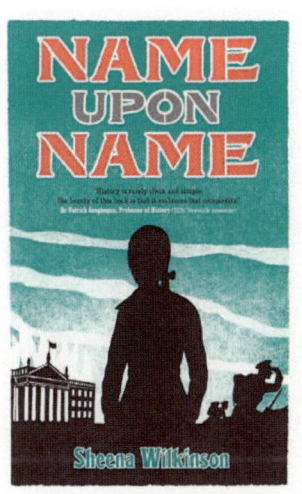

Star by Star is my favourite of my own novels, and it's been my most successful, critically and commercially. But it was so nearly never written. I'd loved writing my first historical novel, *Name Upon Name* (2015), set in 1916, which I had the pleasure of sharing with you here in 2016, and I was keen to write another. But I didn't want to write one on spec – far too much work! – and in the meantime I had written *Street Song* – very gritty, very contemporary – inspired by my lifelong love of music – definitely a book of which Miss Annersley would disapprove. It's sex, drugs and rock'n'roll – literally.

Both my agent and I were confident that *Street Song* would be my first book to crack the UK market. Everything until then had done well in Ireland, got great reviews and sometimes won prizes, but this book, we felt, was more commercial. It would be my breakthrough.

It wasn't. Nobody wanted it – too many Miss Annersleys on editorial boards maybe?

I'd always suspected Little Island, my Irish publishers, wouldn't like *Street Song*, but we had sent it to them as courtesy. I was right: they hated it. The email from my publisher, Siobhán Parkinson, was very clear on that. I wasn't too disappointed – just a week before, the book had been sold to a Scottish publisher (who did very well with it) – and when I read the next paragraph, my heart sang. Don't think this is a consolation prize, Siobhán wrote, but we would like you to write another historical novel, about the 1918 General Election, when women were granted the vote for the first time.

It was a dream commission. All my favourite things in one book, and my chance to write an overtly feminist, political novel, something I'd always wanted to do. I set myself the challenge of writing a book that would be accessible to a bright twelve year old, but that would have plenty to offer the adult reader too. Siobhán's only request was that the heroine be 'a feisty, kick-ass feminist' – which was great, but I knew she – Stella – had to work as a character born in 1903.

And what kind of fifteen-year-old girl would be passionately interested in an election? The novel had to have the 1918 General Election as its climax, and I had to make the reader really care about it. Which meant Stella had to care too. But I couldn't easily make her a suffragette: she was too young. Most suffragette activity stopped in 1914 when war broke out, and Stella was only eleven. The solution was to make her mother a passionate suffragette, and Stella to have been brought up in that tradition. That also allowed me to make her self-confessedly modern and forward-thinking. And when I killed off her mother, it gave her even more reason to care about the vote her mother had fought so hard for, to fulfil her mother's legacy:

But she wasn't around to fight any more, and I was stuck on the edge of a cliff with an old lady, a consumptive widow, an unknown aunt and a pert maid who despised me. I didn't see much chance of changing society.

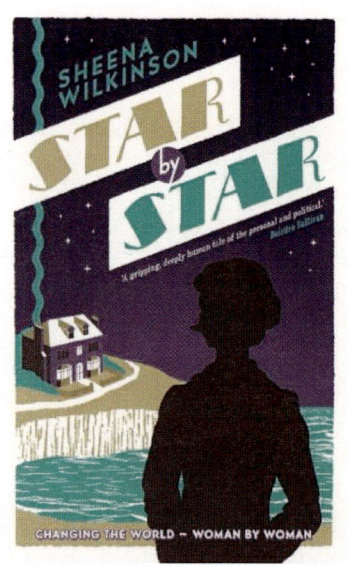

It's not a school story – Stella has left school and is at a commercial college. But like a schoolgirl heroine, she is sent away to an unfamiliar environment, and she struggles with the contrast between the bustle of her hometown, Manchester and the quiet Irish seaside town where her chances to change the world seem very limited. Though I don't think it's a massive spoiler to say that she does change things for one or two people.

You'll all be familiar with the Wild Irish Girl trope in schoolgirl fiction of the late 19th and early 20th C. The WIG is generally emotional, fiery, brave and impetuous – perfect qualities for my heroine. However, Stella comes from England to Ireland, and disrupts a small community – her aunt's women's boarding house – with her passion. I enjoyed playing with that cliché and inverting it.

Funnily enough I was most looking forward to writing about the flu pandemic. In real life I am horribly squeamish – please don't even cough near me - but I do love a good illness on the page, the gorier the better. I was terribly disappointed when I finally tracked down *A Head Girl's Difficulties* (or rather, Gill Bilski did the tracking down) to find how lacking in detail it was about the diphtheria epidemic. And I always love the near-death scenes in the Chalet School.

54

But in *Star by Star* people really do die: they have to if I'm to keep faith with the history. Between spring 1918 and spring 1919, the flu killed at least fifty million worldwide, including 20,000 in Ireland. On one day in October 1918, 60 people dropped dead in the street in London. It was a challenge to suggest the horror of that time, when people really didn't know if this strange illness was 'only' flu, and theories abounded – a judgement from God because of the outrage of four years of war; another plague. Stella can't bear this talk because it reminds her so painfully of her mother's death. In this scene, a young VAD, Kit, has joined the household, and the talk is, inevitably, of flu:

'It blazed through my last place… like a dose of salts,' Kit said. 'At one point I was the only nurse for thirty men, all coughing and vomiting and screaming. Writhing in their own filth. Turning blue and dying. I've been a VAD for two years but this was like – I don't know, some medieval pestilence.' (…)
Mrs Phillips drew her scarf tighter round her neck, as if protecting herself… 'It's a judgement. It has to be. Mankind has gone mad – all this killing, and the Lord has sent his vengeance.'
Turning blue. Writhing. Dying.
'The war may have something to do with it,' Kit said. 'All those men holed up together in stinking trenches. They say the rats are as big as cats, and all those bodies lying unburied—'
Miss McKay put her hand on Kit's arm. 'Pas devant l'enfant,' she murmured. 'She's gone a wee bit green. And who can blame her.'

Who indeed!

And of course the whole book is suffused with the war and its aftermath.

Maybe because I grew up in Belfast during the Troubles, I've always been particularly interested in post-conflict eras – what was life like for people whose lives were changed for ever – which basically meant most people even if not directly affected. In *Star by Star* we have two former soldiers, Sandy and Charlie, and Kit the aforementioned VAD nurse. Even in quiet Cuanbeg, Stella can't escape the war: "*All over the town, just like in Manchester, people were in mourning. Even when they didn't wear black, you saw it in their faces.*" And: "*Cycling home … I wondered what it would be like when all the soldiers finally came home. Millions of men walking round with horrible memories. Millions of women making allowances.*"

I was asked to write a book about an election, but it turned out to be about so much more:

'The war, the flu, independence … There's so much going on. You can't get your head round all of it at once.'
'Like the sky,' I said. 'You can only grasp it star by star.'
I thought of all the women voting today, every vote brightening the future, like stars pricking through the darkness one by one.

Star by Star isn't exactly a sequel to **Name upon Name** – each book is standalone, with a different main character. Sequels aren't always easy to sell and although *Name upon Name* was well reviewed, it didn't set the world alight commercially. But I do like connections between books – from Elsie Oxenham to Jilly Cooper, I love the sense of an interconnected world. So Helen and Sandy, main characters in *Name upon Name*, are important characters in *Star by Star*. And I'm delighted to say that Little Island have commissioned a third historical novel. *Hope against Hope* is set in a girls' hostel in Belfast in 1921 – think Angela Brazil with rioting and sewing machines. It's due out next year, and maybe I'll be invited back to tell you all about it. The main character is someone from *Star by Star* – I planted her just in case…If you read the book and can accurately spot who she is, let me know!

Bang, Bang, Bang! Then Give Three Cheers For Good King George's Royal Engineers: Eric Linklater, War, and "The Wind on the Moon"
Elizabeth Williams

I first read *The Wind on the Moon*, when I was about eight. I don't know why I picked it off the library shelf - it didn't have 'mystery' or 'adventure' or 'pony' in the title. I was fascinated, even though, probably because I was reading it silently and independently, a lot of it was difficult to understand. I took it back to the library and remembered it as a rather special book but didn't come across it again. Later, there it was in the school library where I was teaching, unread for many years, I imagine, before I found it. I re-read it immediately and eventually began to read it aloud to my class of ten and eleven year olds. They loved it and I loved doing the voices. It became one of my very favourite 'reading aloud' books. A few years ago I chose to write about *The Wind on the Moon* for a children's literature course and found both the book and the author more and more fascinating.

Eric Linklater, self- styled Scottish (and especially Orcadian) author was born in Wales in 1899, leaving Cardiff in about 1913 for Aberdeen. His father was an Orcadian sea captain, his Mother half Swedish and half English. He spent many childhood holidays in Orkney; his father owning a small cottage there. When the First World War broke out and after his father died following the sinking of his ship by the German Navy, Linklater tried to join the army but he was too young.

He finished school then started to study medicine at Edinburgh University. After adding a year to his age and finding a way to amend his medical record to make his eyesight seem better, the eighteen-year-old entered the First World War as a private in the Black Watch. Perhaps surprisingly with his poor eyesight he became a sufficiently good shot to become a marksman and was quickly promoted. He endured the mud and horror of the trenches, then was badly wounded in the head.

I was hit on the head by a German bullet. I fell unconscious on friendless ground but quickly recovered [...] and with some difficulty made my way to a Regimental Aid Post. There I was encouraged to take a closer look at my helmet.....There was a neat little hole where the bullet had made its entrance; there was a large and jagged hole where the bullet, flattened and disappointed by the density of my Nordic skull, had forced an exit and gone off in the general direction of Ypres. With the determination of the slightly insane I kept possession of my helmet, and I still have it.

Linklater was in hospital for quite a few months leaving him with a permanent deep groove in the back of his head. He didn't return to France. In 1919 he resumed university, changing course to English, then he began his career as a writer of novels, history books, biography, political articles and plays. His experiences had not given him a distaste for the army and he continued to be active as an amateur soldier. Perhaps his injury and his experiences in the trenches always affected him. He was a strange man, and, reading his biography, rather difficult to like, especially in his attitude to his wife.

By the nineteen thirties Eric Linklater was a very successful writer. He married Marjorie and in 1934 his daughter Sally was born followed by another daughter Kristin in 1936. He based himself and his family at Merkister on Orkney. He was politically active, a member of the Scottish Nationalist Party, even standing for parliament. However he was a committed supporter of the king and the empire, hardly mainstream for the party! Eventually he became frustrated by the party's lack of direction, leaving it in 1933 with the jibe '*You'll make nothing of this until you bring the English in to run it for you*'. He travelled widely as a writer and journalist, and was a vocal opponent of Fascism and Communism.

Linklater said that 'Nazism' was '*a loathsome regime*' as early as 1934. Because of his views his books were eventually banned in Germany, something that he was very proud of. His reaction to being told that his publishers should not use a Jewish translator for a German edition of one of his novels was scathing. He wrote to Rupert Hart-Davis. '*If GovertsVerlag refuse to employ him simply because he is a Jew, you can tell them to stuff a large bag of tin swastikas up their fundamental orifices...*' In 1938 the Munich agreement filled him with horror: '*I can't see the advantage [...] of peace with ignominy. For years past I have said –and believed- that Hitlerism is an evil thing, and for years past I have wished that this country would make a stand against it.* '

Eric had retained his link with the Territorial Army, and on the outbreak of war he was immediately commissioned - Captain E.R. Linklater, Royal Engineers - a Sapper in name at least. By November 1939 he was Major Linklater, now forty and involved in the fortification of Scapa Flow. His talents, and his lack of sapping potential, were eventually recognised by the

Ministry of Information / War Office and he began to write morale boosting articles and radio broadcasts.

In the summer of 1942 he was sent home to his family for six weeks to write a new radio piece. Marjorie had a new baby, Magnus, and Eric was asked to take his two daughters out for a walk. His version is that he thought that it was going to rain, but Marjorie disagreed. Without an umbrella he set off in full uniform, complete with swagger cane and Sally and Kristin, aged seven and five. They didn't want to go but for a mile or two the sun shone and the two girls seemed to enjoy themselves. But then it began to rain – heavily - and they were more than a mile from home. According to Linklater they wailed loudly. There were lots of people about, carrying umbrellas, and Linklater felt that they sympathised with the soaking girls and disapproved of him, imagining even that they suspected him of hitting his daughters with his swagger stick. In desperation he began to tell them a story...'*about two little girls who were very naughty because of something that happened on the moon.*' The crying became quieter and eventually stopped as they listened to his story. I can imagine him changing the voice for each character. When he arrived home to little sympathy from Marjorie, he thought that there were possibilities to this story and immediately began to take notes. Over the next two years he developed this tale until it became ***The Wind on the Moon***.

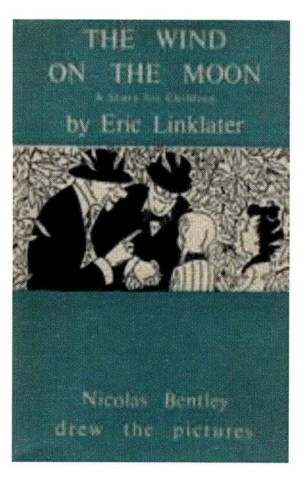

Dinah and Dorinda, the main protagonists, are obviously based on Sally and Kristin. Major Palfrey, about to set off on a dangerous mission, is Major Linklater. Sally Linklater remembers her father:

'*Reprimand was at times unstinted. My father never raised a finger to punish us physically, but his tongue was formidable. His favourite threat was "I'll beat you to within an inch of your life!" and when he was really angry this became "I'll beat you to within an inch of your life with rusty barbed wire." I truly believed he would.*'

Major Palfrey, as he is leaving in the first chapter of ***The Wind on the Moon***' is wondering how to ensure that his daughters will behave:

'"*Would it help you*" said their father, "*if I were to give you a thrashing before I go?*"

He often talked about thrashing them, because he himself, when he was a boy, had been beaten every week, and he thought it had done him good. But he was too tender-hearted to put his belief into practice.'

I am convinced that he invented the ineffectual character of Mrs Palfrey to lampoon Marjorie, blaming her for his situation as he endures his sodden journey home. For example the children (because the Wind on the Moon has got into their hearts and they feel an unstoppable urge to be naughty) are

58

eating huge amounts of food. They demand more pudding: *'"You've had far too much already" said their mother, "but I suppose I must give in to you"'*

Perhaps he made up the next part of the story on the family walk in the rain. Eventually Dinah and Dorinda get so fat that the local children, led by the evil Catherine Crumb, imagine that they are balloons and prick them with pins. The sisters cry and cry until they look like matchsticks and Catherine Crumb suggests striking them. He might have had time to tell his daughters about Dinah and Dorinda's attempted revenge, changing into kangaroos with the help of the local witch Mrs Grimble in order to give Catherine a good kicking, but instead being captured and put in a zoo where they meet, talk to, and free the animals that want to leave, but I can't think that he got much further. He must have used the voices of his characters, like Constable Drum

'In the Kings name! ...
If you do not behave yourselves I shall put you all in prison. Let there be no more rioting, roistering, brawling or biting, barking or fighting. Be good people and go to your homes. Whoever is late for his luncheon shall feel the weight of my truncheon! God save the King.'

And in the zoo, solving the mystery of the missing ostrich egg, Marie Louise the llama, who had lived for a long time in Lyon, says. 'Well, *whenever there is a crime in France the policemen always say* 'Cherchez la femme,' And the gnu who says 'Pooh pooh! .... Tell us, do', 'ah who?', 'Coo!' and 'Adieu' and not much else. But the book is not just an entertaining tale to read aloud - this is 1942, and the country is fighting for freedom. As the golden puma says *'Life without freedom is a poor, poor thing.'*

After his six weeks at home Linklater left for the Faeroes, travelling back to Orkney on an armed trawler in a small convoy, towing a crippled tanker. He must have had plenty of time to think and write, and perhaps entertained himself by developing his children's book. Later in 1942 Eric Linklater's job was to write *'features calculated to put across the army in the right light'*. His patriotic discussion plays include this line

The Allied nations, being in agreement about whom they are fighting against, will probably win the war. But unless they are in equal agreement about the cause they are fighting for, they will not be able to make a good and fruitful peace. And I ask you again, does a fruitful cause exist?

Linklater discusses what improvements need to be made post war. Rabelais' final words are: *'Let them be given what you in England were given at Runnymede, a charter of rights and justice: a great Charter for children!'* In October Linklater was sent to Gibraltar, then to Tangiers, and in 1944 on to Algiers and Italy, a country and people that he had loved before the war.

As **The Wind on the Moon** develops it becomes a book about freedom in all its aspects. When Dinah and Dorinda release the animals from the zoo not many of them choose to leave. Most just like to have the freedom to decide. To the puma and her friend the magnificent silver falcon, freedom means roaming freely. The puma says, *'All last night I walked in the forest with the smell of the trees and the rich ground in my nostrils and the darkness was beautiful,'* then describes how she hunted a deer and made her kill. And the falcon says, *'Freedom is worth all the peril in the world, freedom's the noblest thing, we live at ease who freely live.'*

But there are less obvious freedoms. Linklater believes that education should involve freedom. In a letter to his daughter Kristin soon after she was born, he said

'You must learn to sail a boat, for that is a very great joy. And to swim, for that is useful if the boat capsized. And to catch fish, for that is invaluable if you swim ashore to a desert island. In fact you are going to learn an enormous number of things.'

Education is a major theme in Linklater's patriotic plays. In the play **Socrates Asks Why**, Voltaire argues that children should be taught

'...language as an instrument of pleasure....history...that will convince them that they are growing things and part of a greater thing that is also growing' and should be given *'their rights: right of shelter and food, of health and joy, of growth and teaching'*.

The **Wind on the Moon** enlarges on this theme. Miss Serendip, the governess, expounds pointless fact after pointless fact, but real education takes place when the children escape into the Forest of Weal with the puma and the falcon.

They learned to see things....They learned to know, by the smell of the wind and the look of the sky, whether tomorrow was going to be fine or foul. They learned... to be interested in everything they saw

or heard and because of that they even learned something from Miss Serendip's dreary lessons.
But they learned neither Music nor Dancing, because Mr Casimir Corvo, who had taught them both these subjects, was still in prison.

Mr. Hobson and Mr. Jobson

Here Linklater is satirizing another aspect of freedom, the imperfect workings of the English legal system. Mr Hobson and Mr Jobson, lawyers, take clients' money but have already decided who will win or lose, winning cases on alternate days. Poor Mrs Taper is innocent of the theft of a pair of stockings. She should be found Not Guilty, because it is a Thursday, but the judge, in a summing up worthy of the Jeremy Thorpe case, says *'If you decide that Mrs Taper is guilty, then the wretched woman will go to prison, as she so richly deserves. If you decide she is Not Guilty, then I shall have to set her free, and she'll continue to go round the country stealing silk stockings wherever she can find them'*

The jury, which includes Mr Casimir Corvo, had all decided which way to vote at the beginning and hadn't listened. They split evenly and refuse to reconsider. Mr Justice Rumple sends them all to prison until they reach a verdict, but the jury consider their freedom to make up their minds more important than physical freedom and refuse to give in. They are only released when the judge is persuaded to change his mind (because not changing it, like not changing his clothes, is insanitary).

Mr Casimir Corvo comes from Bombardy. You may remember that Major Palfrey has gone on a hazardous mission. The children's mother receives a bloodstained letter. In fact he has gone to Bombardy, a country ruled by the cruel tyrant Count Hulagu Bloot, and he has been captured and put in a dungeon; *'By good fortune I was wearing winter underclothing at the time of my arrest, so I am quite warm, though the dungeon is unheated '.*

61

Now the story takes a new turn, one in which magic takes no part, except that Dinah and Dorinda can still talk to the puma and the falcon. Dinah, Dorinda, Mr Corvo, the puma and the falcon set off to rescue Major Palfrey. Reviewers assumed that Count Hulagu Bloot is an allegory for Hitler. He may be, but Nicholas Bentley, who drew the pictures, doesn't seem to think so. Linklater describes Count Hulagu.

'*Count Hulagu was a middle-aged man with a long yellow face and thick lips the colour of mulberries. His hair grew like stubble in a barley field, he had little greenish glittering eyes, a long nose with a wart on it, and whiskers grew out of his ears.*'

Surely this is more Mussolini! Eric Linklater had a great affection for Italy, where he and Marjorie had lived before the war. He wrote his adult novel **Private Angelo** at the end of the war, depicting the horrors endured by the Italian people.

Mr Corvo says of the capital:

'*I was born in Gliedermannheim. It is a beautiful town in a beautiful country, but now it is ruled by a cruel man, a tyrant and all my people are suffering as never before.*' He also says: '*We Bombards are not a cruel people. It is only that infamous Count Hulagu who makes my people behave so badly.*'

They travel to Bombardy hidden among furniture being delivered to Count Hulagu Bloot. Count Hulagu's house reflects his vileness, with pictures of people being tortured, stuffed animals and: '*In one corner there were some dumb-bells, a skipping–rope, and a Sandow developer for the muscles; and in another corner a bookcase with a book in it called* **How to Make Friends and Influence People**.' I would think that this sort of detail would be lost on young children, so who was Eric Linklater writing this for? I suspect that he was amusing himself. He must have been spending a lot of time alone, travelling in some danger around Europe. There is a lot of detail that I missed, even reading the book aloud. For instance, there is the language of Bombast, which I just enjoyed the sound of, as I read it aloud

The rescue party manage to get into the castle, stay overnight in the Count's suite and Mr Corvo leaves a note for the butler. Here it is: '*Gribn unjerdee tevi. Chi issu resh grunhy. Gribn chess fosue, telpyn skepc, chum feekfa, satto, titsanpipse, lamrameda und rubeer, dun eni fabseeket* '. Can you translate it? Fortunately Linklater provides a translation, which assists us: '*Bring breakfast quickly. Bring six eggs, plenty bacon, much coffee, toast rolls, marmalade and butter, and one beefsteak.*'

They set off to follow a secret passage to the dungeons. A notice reads XUA TOCCASH (to the dungeons). Unfortunately they leave a trail of peppermint creams and just as they find Major Palfrey, Count Hulagu Bloot captures them. He makes a speech.

'Uqi esi stee chi refai ont assi dun chi refai ont reac. Amsi vendelity esi stee rusovel dun masi nov el Nagsali Palfrey Laprouce chis sifa esi nemi sornireps. Setse eni nov nemi boshbie a renti meth El remo el rerimer! Ehri esi stee, dunehri esi nezratted dun tro nulit esi stee troms! Ha-ha-ha.'

Now Mr Corvo only gives a rough translation.

'He doesn't know who we are, and doesn't care. We are his prisoners and that is enough for him. He likes to have prisoners. He collects prisoners and the more he has the better he is pleased.'

Janice Brown has helpfully provided a dictionary at the end of this article. I can only think that Linklater is entertaining himself. If I can't do it, surely eight year olds can't make much of it.

So how do they escape? Well, here the author introduces characters with an allusion that only he and a small section of military personnel will understand. Two little old men in patched and faded blue trousers appear through the floor. They are Mr Stevens and Notchy Knight and they sing:

'Sap, sap, sap, sap, sap a little more
Sap and sap till your bones are sore!
We sap all night and we sap all day,
And that's how we go ubique'
……..then
'Bang, bang, bang! Then give three cheers
For Queen Victoria's Royal Engineers!'
"Good Heavens!" said Major Palfrey. "It can't be true!"'

But it is. Two sappers have lost direction while tunnelling during the Crimean War and emerge in Bombardy. They are Royal Engineers, (motto *Ubique* - everywhere for those of us who did not learn Latin at school.) Those of you who are concentrating hard and have good memories will remember that Linklater was a major in the Royal Engineers. Their names are from a regimental song from the Boer War. How many people who read **The Wind on the Moon** would understand the allusion? Any? I keep intending to contact the Royal Engineers to ascertain whether they know about it.

Of course Count Hulagu is killed and the children escape, but this is wartime and reality insists that one major character has to die. Freedom is not bought easily. Sorry about the spoiler, but the book has been around since 1944. The beautiful, gentle and gallant golden puma saves them all at the cost of her life. Her last words are: *'You gave me what I love above all things. You gave me a little while of freedom. Have I repaid you?'*

The two old Sappers, after having found out that Queen Victoria is dead, *'just go on sapping'* singing *'Bang, bang, bang! Then give three cheers For Good King George's Royal Engineers'*. When the remainder of the party return home the falcon reports that the people of Bombardy have set up a great monument to the puma:

IN EVER GRATEFUL MEMORY
OF
THE GOLDEN PUMA
WHO SLEW COUNT HULAGU BLOOT
AND FREED US
FROM HIS TYRANNY

The book finished, all Linklater had to do now was get it published, and he wanted a quality edition. As Girlsown fans will know, paper in wartime was in short supply, He was a very successful author, and he wrote to Jonathan Cape, his publishers, *'I think I really do realise something of a publisher's difficulties in wartime…If you haven't enough paper to keep in print books that would sell, you can't have very much to speculate on books that might sell.'* So he took **The Wind on the Moon** to Macmillan, who produced a high quality book. I particularly like the pictures by Nicholas Bentley. Linklater said: *'It was successful far beyond my expectation, and still brings me a little comfort. Those dear children, bellowing their anger… How grateful I was!'*

In November 1945 The Library Association chose **The Wind on the Moon** to win the Carnegie medal as the best children's book of the previous year. After the war Linklater wrote more books, including two for children. *Private Angelo*, later made into a film, a searing adult account of the experiences of an Italian soldier, perhaps best mirrors the fictional Major Palfrey's feelings towards the people of Bombardy.

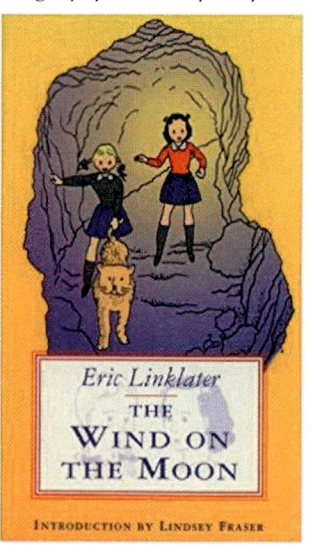

<u>Bombast to English Translation with thanks to Janice Brown</u>
A=a (F) to
Amsi=mais (F)=but
Assi=sais (F)=know
Beah=habe (G)=have
Beeli=libe (G) =love
Boshbie=hobbies
Chess=sechs (G)=six
Chi=ich(G)=I
Chum=much
Dun=und (G)=and
Ehri=hier9G()=here
El=le(F)=the
El Nagsali=Le Anglais (F) =the Englishman
Eni=ein (G)=one
Esi=sie (G) =you
Fabseekat=beefsteak
Feekfa=kaffee (G)=coffee

64

Fosue=oeufs (F)=eggs
Glon=long
Gribn=bring
Hundossat=thousands
Issu=suis(F)=am
Lamrameda =marmalade
Masi=amis (F) =friends
Meth=them
Nemi=mein (G) =my
Nezratted=attendrez(F)=wait for
Nov=v0n (G) =of
Nulit=until
Ont=not
Reac=care
Refai=faire (F)=do
Remo=more
Renti=tenir(F)=hold
Rerimer=merrier
Resh=sehr(G)=very
Rithenn=thinner
Rubeer=buerre (F)=butter

Rusovel=voleurs (F) thieves
Satto=toast
Setse=esset(G)=eat?
Sifa=fais (F) make
Skepc=speck (G)=bacon
Sornireps=prisoners
Stee=etes (F) =are
Tavan=avant(F)=before
Tevi=vite(F)=quickly
Toccash=cachots (F)=dungeons
Troms=mort(F)=dead
Unjerdee=dejeuner(F)=dinner
Uqi=qui (F) =who
Vendelity=evidently
Zeers=serez(F)=will be
Telpyn=plenty
Titsanpipse=petitpains (F)=rolls
Tro=rot
Xua=aux (F)=to the
Zeers=serez(F)=will be

We couldn't work out any translation of laprouce or setse that really worked in context. Perhaps you can!

Girls of the Great War
A Picture in Words and Music
28th July 2018
Compiled by Sally Dore

The theme of this year's conference was chosen in commemoration of the ending of the First World War in 1918. Tonight we will be painting a picture in words and music of the lives of girls who lived through the Great War, ending with *Jerusalem*, the third of the songs this evening in which you are warmly invited to join us if you wish. Our very grateful thanks to our readers and musicians.

Readers: Anne-Bénédicte Damon, Sally Dore, Jenny Hill, Betula O'Neill, Rosalind Russell, Sheena Wilkinson

Soloist: Rosalind Russell
Accompanist: Marjory Williamson

Songs

1. ***Keep the Home Fires Burning*** *(1914)* (please join in the chorus)
Music by Ivor Novello, words by Lena Gilbert Ford.
Ivor Novello was only 21 when he wrote this instant hit which captured the mood of the moment. By 1916 over a million copies of the sheet music had been sold. Novello's service in the Royal Navy Air Service ended after he crashed two aeroplanes, but he later had a very successful career as an actor,

writer and composer. Lena Ford was an American divorcee living in London with her son when she wrote these lyrics. Both were killed in a German air raid in March 1918.

2. *Danny Boy* (1913)
Words by Frederick Weatherly, music the traditional Irish folk tune the Londonderry Air
Although this was written by Bristolian Frederick Weatherly in 1913, it remained extremely popular during the war. Weatherly was both a successful barrister, a KC in fact, and a prolific lyricist of over 1300 popular songs, of which *Danny Boy* is now the most famous.

3. *Pack Up Your Troubles* (1915)
(please join in)
Music by Felix Powell, words by George Henry Powell
Felix Powell was an army staff sergeant, while George Henry Powell became a conscientious objector. The song was extremely well known, and Wilfred Owen used "Smile, Smile, Smile" as the title of one of his poems later in the war.

4. *England (This Royal Throne of Kings)* (1916)
This is a paraphrase of John of Gaunt's famous speech in Shakespeare's *King Richard II*, set to music by Sir Hubert Parry. It is little known today, but was still being sung by Chalet School girls (and presumably others) in the Second World War. Prof Jeremy Dibble of Durham University, a Parry scholar, noted that *England* is about more than just flying the flag - 'its rousing tune expresses a sense of vision, self-sacrifice and hope, typical of Parry's own outlook.'

5. *The Roses of Picardy* (1916) *A recording of Ernest Pike made in 1917*
Words by Frederick Weatherly, music by Haydn Wood
This is another of Weatherly's hugely popular songs, one of the big hits of the War, selling a steady 50,000 copies per month, and making the composer over £10,000. This contemporary recording enables us to hear the very singing that our WWI girls would have heard.

6. *Speedwell* (1918)
Music by Morfydd Owen, words by Atwyth Eversley
It seems fitting to have a song by this prolific young Welsh composer in the centenary year of her death. Morfydd Owen was only 28 when she died, following chloroform poisoning suffered during an operation.

7. Jerusalem *(1916)* (please join in)
Words by William Blake, music by Sir Hubert Parry
The Poet Laureate, Robert Bridges, felt that Blake's poem could "brace the spirit of the nation [to] accept with cheerfulness all the sacrifices necessary" during war. He asked Parry to write a stirring setting that all could "take up and join in", to be premiered at a "Fight for Right" campaign meeting in 1916. Parry was pleased with his setting for organ and voice, but he later began to have misgivings about the Fight for Right movement and withdrew his support in 1917, at which point the song might have been withdrawn altogether. It was "saved" by Millicent Garrett Fawcett, leader of the National Union of Women's Suffrage Societies. With its idealistic words and stirring setting, it had become popular in the suffrage movement, and she asked Parry if it could be used at a Suffrage Demonstration Concert in March 1918. Parry was delighted, and orchestrated it for that occasion. He also granted her further request that it should become the women voters' hymn, and he gifted the copyright to the NUWSS. When the NUWSS was wound up in 1928, Parry's executors reassigned the copyright to the Women's Institutes, where it remained until it came into the public domain in 1968.

Readings are taken from:
Unpublished diary, 1912-18, Helen Lindsay
https://www.edinburghnews.scotsman.com/news/people/diary-shows-schoolgirl-s-experience-of-war-1-2039360
Phyllis McPhilemy; May Baldwin 1915
Spoilt Cynthia at School; May Baldwin 1917
A Patriotic Schoolgirl; Angela Brazil 1918
Colston's Girls' School, Bristol, *School Magazine*, Summer 1918
Sunday Times, 28th July 1918
Birmingham Daily Post, 27th July 1918
King Edward VI High School for Girls, Birmingham, 1883-1925. Compiled by Winifred I. Vardy (Mrs E.W. Candler) 1928
Redland High School [Bristol]; M.G. Shaw; 1932
The Story of Walthamstow Hall: Material collected by Elsie Pike & arranged by Constance E. Curryer 1938
Myself When Young; Daphne du Maurier 1978
The Pebbled Shore; Elizabeth Longford 1986
Fighting All the Way; Barbara Castle 1993

Girls of the Great War

Betula
From the Sunday Times of the 28th July 1918: German Ace Brought Down
On Thursday night Lt Walter Avery of Columbus, Ohio brought down the noted German "ace", Captain Mendkoff. The German plane manoeuvred and tried to fool Avery with tricks, which failed. After twenty minutes Avery got on the German plane's tail, damaged it, and forced it to land behind the American lines, and brought in the German "ace". The latter, when told he had been out-fought by an American in his first battle, got enraged, sulked, and refused to talk.

Sheena Other headlines from the 28th July 1918:
Rosalind An Aeroplane Parachute – Designer's Death on first Descent
Sally New Meat Rations – Vegetables more plentiful
Jenny Turks and Bulgars Come to Blows – Fighting along ceded railway – Quarrel between Germany's Dupes
Anne-Benedicte Premier's War message – novel method of publication
Sheena Alleged Train Outrage – Story of Chloroformed Handkerchief
Betula India's Future – Mr Montagu on Home Rule
Anne-Benedicte Thonville Raid – Huge conflagration started
Jenny No Teachers' Strike – bonus proposal to cost £865,000 a year
Betula Appalling U-boat Crime – Four Seamen Drowned – Placed on Submarine and Submerged
Rosalind British Raid Cattaro – Damage to Aerodrome and U-Boat Base.

Sally
Tonight we are hoping to create an impression of what life was like for girls a century ago as – **we** now know, although they did not - the Great War was drawing to its close. The experience of civilians at home during the First World War has not impinged on our consciousness in the way the Home Front of the second war has, but many of the things we associate with that experience, such as food rationing and air raids, were similar in the earlier conflict. We have extracts from memoirs, histories, newspapers, fact and fiction, music and songs, to paint a picture for you. There will be three songs which you are warmly invited to join in.

In 1932, M.G. Shaw recalled:
"The years of the Great War are still vivid to all who lived through them, and I know that for many Old Girls [of Redland High School], when they think of Miss Shekleton, her picture comes back in the setting of those years. No one who was there can ever forget her enthusiasm and her sympathy. She was determined that the School and every member of it should do their share. We educated Belgian Refugees; we abolished prizes and gave money to war funds; we had weekly collections into which most of our pocket money went. During one term alone we subscribed £67 10s for the Star and Garter fund. We had working parties at which we cut out shirts, sewed, knitted (and talked!). We collected – what didn't we collect? – all our rooms were full of collections. There were clothes, old tins, silver paper, silver thimbles for the Ambulance Fund, foxgloves leaves and horse chestnuts (for mysterious conversion into gunpowder we believed). Well do I remember a huge sack of horse chestnuts, brought one Monday morning by two eager collectors, bursting (accidentally, of course!) outside the office door, and the ardour with which the whole School ran after the rolling chestnuts.

"The School joined the Patriotic Union of Girls' Schools and offered its services to the Bristol Branch of the Red Cross, and through them furnished all towels and cloths for the Extra Enteric Ward of the Bristol Royal Infirmary, several hundred articles in all. We entertained seventy wounded soldiers to tea in the hall and the Junior School acted *Snow White and the Dwarfs*, which was much appreciated. Two huge trunks and twenty-five large parcels of clothes were dispatched for the Belgian Refugees; …blue and khaki mufflers for the Navy and the Army; books, cigarettes, stamped envelopes and paper for men at the front. At Christmas-time the Cookery

Class made plum puddings and sent them out to our popular Inspector, Colonel G.H. Cookson, for the men in his regiments. We ran a War Savings Association in School; we adopted a prisoner of war and sent him parcels regularly. We went forth in bands armed with spades, shovels and brooms, and swept the snow from all the roads adjoining us! A choir was formed in connection with the National Carol League and went out at night singing carols; Miss Shekleton herself held the lantern and led the choir, which made a large sum of money in aid of St Dunstan's.

"I may seem to be writing very lightly of these years, but that is only because the real memory of the time is too deep for words. The war drew us all very close together at Redland, and the Intercession Services taken by Miss Shekleton and so well attended proved a real source of help and comfort to those in sorrow and anxiety. One who was a girl in the School at the time said of Miss Shekleton: "No one will ever forget the joy in her face at the Armistice Service on 11th November 1918, as she sang, 'Praise the Lord, ye heavens adore Him.'"

Above: Miss Shekleton and her staff in 1915
Song: Keep the Home Fires Burning
<u>Rosalind</u>
Colston's Girls School magazine, Summer Term 1918
War Work
Plain Sewing Section
In the Plain Sewing Section of war work eighteen shirts, seventy-two treasure bags, twelve pairs of flannelette boots, and two dozen handkerchiefs have been made. The shirts – ready cut out – were kindly supplied by S. Nathanael's Branch of the Red Cross Society.

Sheena
Elizabeth Longford:
"Several of my school years were enlivened by the zeppelin raids on London. We were too young to be more than pleasantly startled by the assorted thumps that we could hear from our refuge in the wine cellar. ...
"I was lifted out of bed one night to see a zeppelin caught in searchlights. My father gave us no hint of his vengeful feelings on such occasions, but he wrote to my mother in September 1915 after the German bombs had broken all the glass in the hospital windows around Bloomsbury: 'People who could do such a thing should be exterminated.' It was the idea of an indiscriminate attack from the **air** that in those days shocked so deeply. ...
"My most dramatic and sinister memory of the First World War was purely imaginary. A schoolfriend lived in a street next door to the British Museum in Bloomsbury. She would sometimes ask me to tea on winter evenings, when our great thrill was to hide behind the window curtains and watch the shadow of a German spy signalling from inside the museum to his accomplice outside. To be sure, all we could really see was the reflection on a blind of someone moving in the room opposite, but that was enough. We revelled in eerie speculations, in which German spies and Egyptian mummies were horrifically mingled."

Jenny
"The pupils and mistresses, throwing on their winter coats, which hung in the cloakroom close by, and carrying their rugs, wended their way, as desired, to the gym, which was in the park, down a flight of steps, and practically underground, forming a famous 'dug-out.' They sang their drill-song as they went; and Nanny, [who had been visiting her old charge. Cynthia] having gone to the kitchen to help, followed after she had secured a small flask of brandy and some matches.
'Look at Nanny! She is going to make a night of it,' cried Betty, catching sight of Nanny clutching her little flask and her matches. There was a roar of laughter, for everyone looked upon it as an adventure, and felt in honour bound not to be frightened.
'If I had known we were coming to such a nice room as this, I should not have troubled about the brandy, but it's a thing I never think it right to be without as a medicine,' said Nanny placidly, as she put it on a shelf and began helping to lay the table....

Just as she spoke there was a loud crash, and a cry from some of the girls.
'Come, girls, begin with your supper. We are quite safe here, and we have got to "carry on," like the men at the front. They have this all day and every day,' cried the matron.
[Nanny goes out to find a girl who didn't hear the alarm].
'You are a funny girl, Cynthia. You don't seem a bit upset. Oh!' – for there came another tremendous explosion. But it was not etiquette to talk of bombs, so Betty continued: 'Suppose she does not come back safely?'
Cynthia looked at her. 'It would be a glorious death,' she said quietly, and Betty did not see that she was white to the lips.
'Upon my word,' cried the girl, shuddering, 'you are callous.'
'No, she is not,' put in the matron. 'She is a true soldier's daughter when danger comes near. – Now, girls, if you have finished supper, suppose we have an impromptu concert?'...
Madame, who had recovered her outward composure after the first crash, applauded, and asked for different items; and only the matron, who sat next to her, saw how tightly her hands were clasped together as the strain of the responsibility of all these young lives told upon her...' ...
While the concert was going on the servants were busy arranging the mattresses which were kept in the gymnasium for an emergency like the present, and spreading upon them the rugs the girls had brought. After prayers the whole household lay down, and some of them fell fast asleep.
Spoilt Cynthia at School by May Baldwin

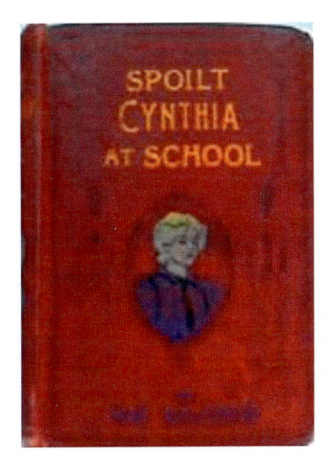

Sheena
Memories of Walthamstow Hall
... There were all kinds of air-raid precautions. If the alarm signal went at night, the girls would be brought hurriedly downstairs, clad in dressing-gown and slippers and each carrying a blanket. I remember one occasion when the little ones were so thrilled with the idea of coming downstairs in the middle of the night that they marched along singing, 'An air raid! An air raid!' to the tune of the Keel Row! In those days every member of the staff had to keep by her in a suit-case £2 in silver so that she could be ready at any moment to flee with her small party of children if the enemy landed in Kent. It all sounds extraordinary and exaggerated now, but on the notice-board in the Staff-room hung what we called 'the rescuer's list': this gave the names of the seven or eight girls allotted to each mistress in case of emergency. And every girl had a small suit-case ready in her bedroom – though the girls did not know the real reason for this.
"How we rejoiced at the end of the war! But it came at a very sad time for the school; almost every girl was either in bed with influenza or downstairs convalescing." ... "Miss Sharpe and Marjorie Milledge developed pneumonia, and no effort could save them."

Song: Danny Boy sung by Rosalind

Betula
Daphne du Maurier
'Singing these songs made us forget to be sad about Uncle Guy, and one day Angela told me that she had overheard someone tell Nurse… that in wartime everyone made eyes at the soldiers.
"What does it mean, making eyes?" I asked her.
"I think it's like this," Angela said, looking sideways out of the corner of her eyes.
"We practised this awhile, and afterwards, when we were walking in Regent's Park, and saw soldiers coming towards us, we used to stare at them sideways, in a squinting sort of way, smiling at the same time. Angela said it was patriotic. But I don't think they noticed, which was disappointing."

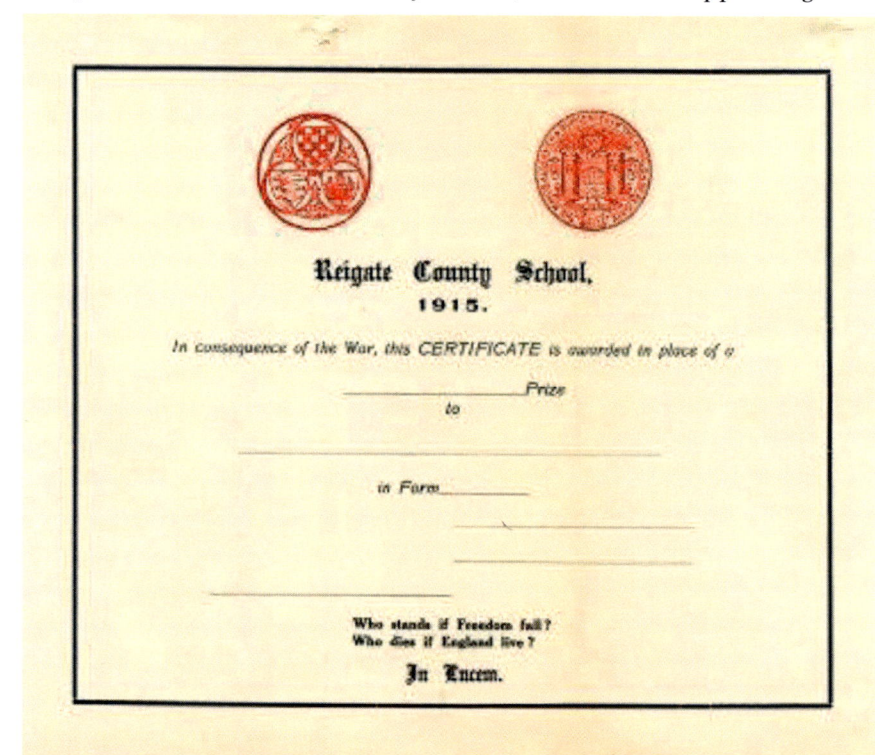

Prize certificate issued in 1915 by Reigate County School for Girls: "In consequence of the War, this Certificate is awarded in place of a _____ Prize… Who stands if Freedom Fall? Who dies if England Live? In Lucem" [In the Light - the school motto]

Sheena
'We have called you all here to ask your votes on the subject of the Christmas prizes,' began Mildred [the Head Girl]… 'As you know, many schools have asked that the prize-money should be given to some fund in connection with the war, and we wish to know what the wishes of the school are,' wound up Mildred and sat down.

'Oh yes, Mildred, let us give the money to the war-fund. We don't want any examinations in war-time,' cried little Doris...
Everybody laughed, and Mildred said with a smile, 'I did not say anything about the examinations, Doris. Of course we shall have them just the same, and we must all try to work our hardest if we give up the prizes. We thought of proposing that we should have certificates instead, stating the fact that in war-time we had no prizes, and that these took their place,' Mildred proceeded to explain.
There was a murmur throughout the room as the girls discussed what Mildred had said; and the Sixth Form let it go on for a time, and then the prefects' bell was rung for silence. ...
'I propose we put it to the vote. Those of you in favour of certificates instead of prizes, hold up your hands.'
Immediately a forest of hands went up.
Mildred looked pleased. 'We will speak to Miss Cox to-night and tell her we shall treasure the certificates as highly as if they were the valuable books they represent.'
'I shall prefer them, as I sha'n't have the bother of reading them. Prizes are always dull,' said one of the Fourth.
'I should not think you have been much troubled that way,' said a candid friend."
From *Phyllis McPhilemy* by May Baldwin

Rosalind
War Work
Knitting Section
No working parties have been held since Christmas, but the work has in no wise suffered from having been done at home, for during the Spring Term thirty-nine pairs of socks were knitted, most of the wool, as in previous terms, having been given by the S. Nathanael's Working Party. Thirty-three pairs of socks were forwarded to the headquarters of the British Red Cross Society in London, while six pairs were handed over to Miss Dixon, who went them to Lieutenant G. Knight, on one of His Majesty's destroyers.
Quite a large number of girls from the Middle as well as the Upper School have joined the section this term, for not only do the older girls hope to send at least twenty pairs of socks to the British Red Cross Society, but the younger members, who have been busily knitting squares to be used as face flannels in the hospitals, expect for forward a considerable number of these to the Darley Dale Hospital in Derbyshire, where Matron assures us they will be much appreciated.

Anne-Benedicte
From the Birmingham Daily Post, 27th July 1918: The Kaiser's Bad Temper
From communications which have reached a well-informed quarter here it is apparently beyond doubt that the conduct of the Kaiser has recently become so unbearable towards Ministers, members of his suite and staff alike, that it is with the greatest difficulty that they can work with him.

Song: Pack Up Your Troubles

Rosalind
War Work

Surgical Section
Since the establishment of the House system, the rival claims of courts and nets have reduced the numbers of those who actually stay for the meetings at school. So much work, however, has been done at home by loyal supporters that hitherto our Hospital friends have been as well supplied as ever. Since our last report we have rolled well into our fourth hundred of bandages, and have already complete 125 T and 55 many-tailed bandages, in addition to some dozens of operating sponges, slings, and several mackintosh pillow-slips. There is a good deal of finished work still to be brought in, including a new type of many-tailed bandage for arm and leg wounds, requested by the Shrewsbury Hospital. We have received very grateful letters from the King George, Gloucester Red Cross, and Shrewsbury Hospitals for the five parcels we have already despatched, and we expect to send off at least two more at the end of term. We hope at the beginning of next term again to welcome the support of many of our old workers who have been too busy with games and examinations to help the cause substantially this term.

Sheena
"It was war-time, and at first I think we felt the pinch most in the matter of food supplies, though Miss Sadler displayed wonderful ingenuity in devising possible dishes from very unusual materials. She gave us jam made of carrot and rhubarb, or carrot and tomato, or date and rhubarb, sugar being unobtainable for jam. And as meat was so scarce we had usually some kind of stew with haricot beans, potatoes and other vegetables, served up in soup-plates and eaten with spoon and fork. The morning porridge was of extremely coarse meal, and I remember one girl saying grimly as she tasted it: 'These husks do bring the war home to one.'
Staff memory of Walthamstow Hall

Betula
The Food Queue (with apologies to Lord Tennyson)
Half a yard, half a yard,
Half a yard onward,
All in a queue for food
    Stood the six hundred.
Forth reeled a hungry maid,
"Charge for the door!" she said:
Into the grocer's shop
Rushed the six hundred.

"Forward, the Food Brigade!"
Was there a soul dismay'd?
Yes, for the grocer knew
    Someone had blunder'd.
His not to make reply,
His not to tell them why
There was no lard to buy –
Into the grocer's shop
    Rushed the six hundred.

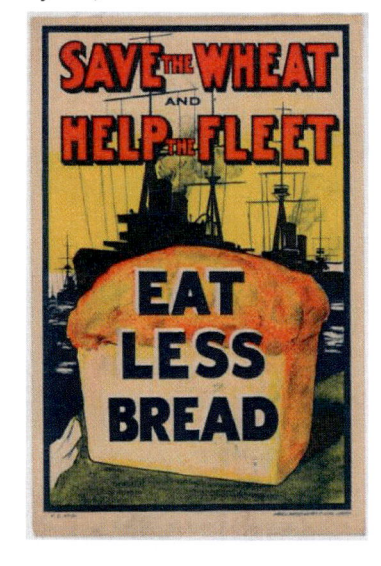

Policemen to right of them,
Specials to left of them,
Grocer in front of them,
    Threatened and thundered:
Stormed at by policemen strong,
Boldly they rushed along,
Into the grocer's shop,
Hungry and seething throng,
Rushed the six hundred.

Flash'd then their fists all bare,
Flash'd as they turned in air,
Punching the policeman there,
Charging a grocer while
    All the world wonder'd:
Armèd with bricks and coke
Right through the line they broke:
Policeman and Special
Reel'd from umbrella's stroke,
Shatter'd and sunder'd.
Then they turned back, but not,
    Not the six hundred.

When can their anger fade?
When be their hunger stayed?
    All the world wonder'd.
Honour the charge they made!
Honour their fateful raid,
    Famishe'd six hundred!

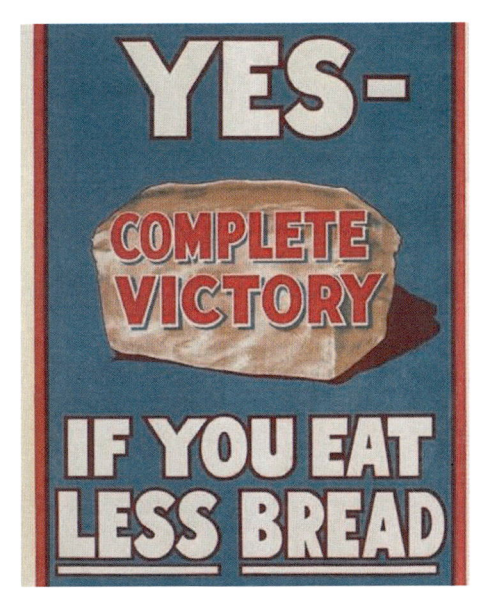

By Jessie Ritblat, (IVa) Colston's Girls' School
Rosalind
War Work
Toy Making
This war work party was continued during the Spring Term, but it became so increasingly difficult to obtain materials which were of any real use for making stuffed animals, that it was decided to give it up at the end of the term. All the members have since joined one of the other war work parties. The few really satisfactory animals which were made are being kept until an opportunity occurs of selling them for the benefit of Red Cross Funds.
Song: England sung by Rosalind
Anne-Benedicte
From the Sunday Times of the 28th July 1918
German Effort to Gain Air Mastery by Hiram Knight
Information that has just reached me from a most reliable source shows that the enemy, who has never been blind to the important part played by aircraft in modern military tactics, is making a serious attempt to gain the mastery of the skies. Despite a very real difficulty in finding sufficient material, and

in sparing enough men for airplane construction, the manufacture of machines of standard types has gone on apace – a fact that is indicated by the stiffening air strength of the enemy.

Sheena
Marjorie lived for news of the war. She devoured the sheets of closely written foreign paper sent home by Father, Bevis and Leonard. She followed all the experiences they described, and tried to imagine them in their dug-outs, on the march, sleeping in rat-ridden barns, or cruising the Channel to sweep mines. When she awoke in the night and heard the rain falling, she would picture the wet trenches, and she often looked at the calm still moon, and thought how it shone alike on peaceful white cliffs and on stained battlefields in Flanders. The aeroplanes that guarded the coast were a source of immense interest at Brackenfield. The girls would look up to see them whizzing overhead. There was a poster at the school depicting hostile aircraft, and they often gazed into the sky with an apprehension that one of the Hun pattern might make its sudden appearance.
A Patriotic Schoolgirl by *Angela Brazil*

Anne-Benedicte
Small ad from the Birmingham Daily Post, 27th July 1918
The Grange, Buxton – School for Girls from 10-19 years. Thorough general education with great attention to health. Elder girls may specialise in Art, Music, Literature or Languages. New Domestic Science Branch for girls over 18. Tennis courts and field for hockey and cricket. Preparation for exams. Principal: Miss L.C. Dodd.

Rosalind
War Work
War Savings Association
A review of this year's work shows very encouraging results. Our old members brought their Christmas presents and Easter gifts, and new members have come forward. This, added to the fact that everyone has tried hard to do her utmost, has made our savings for the two terms amount to over £330, which is more than half the sum of money contributed during the previous eighteen months of our existence.
We celebrated the second anniversary of our foundation in June, and at the same time we found ourselves in the proud position of having purchased 1000 certificates. All War Savings Associations rejoice when they have accomplished this feat, and although it has taken C.G.S. somewhat long to reach the goal, we congratulate our members on having attained it. This does not mean that £1000 has been saved yet for war weapons, and our next effort must be directed towards producing £150, which is the sum now needed to make up that total.
At our first House meetings after the Easter holidays, we thought we might aim to providing the money necessary for a number of machine guns. We have collected enough for two, and are hoping that a third will be added to their number before the end of the term.
House matches, holidays and examinations have caused our members to be a little neglectful at times, and we would take this opportunity of urging them to be loyal to this very important branch of war work.

Betula

The Staff of the King Edward VI High School for Girls in Birmingham put on a melodrama, *The Felonies of Ferolith*, which raised £32 for the Newnham and Girton Unit of the Scottish Women's War Hospital. An old girl recalled: "Mistresses came from the seclusion of the staff room and even dared to act a movie-stage play for the amusement of the school and the benefit of war funds. The play was a real cinema shocker, with all the crudities of the movies scenes and 'close-ups' well emphasised. Who can ever forget the villain on that occasion chasing the heroine down a spiral staircase – the staircase being symbolised on stage by two Assembly room chairs, round and round which the villain and heroine gyrated. It was a glorious skit. The school rocked with laughter and felt that the mistresses were of their own generation. The day after the cinema show the staff had lost none of its dignity and was appreciated all the more."

One of the younger among the audience later recalled:
"To my childish imagination '*Ferolith*' easily surpassed Shakespeare. Miss E. S. Ravenhill was the hero – Sir Mark Tressington; I can well remember how awed we were by her 'plus-fours.' Miss Major and Miss Bacon as Miss Holmes and Miss Watson, famous detective and faithful admirer, delighted the audience, but to the Lower School the greatest feature of the play was the bull – Bill the Bellower – made of Miss Catnach and Miss Bromhead, which bellowed both ends. Imagine our delight when in the excitement of the play Bill lost his hind legs and pranced about the stage in two pieces!"

Helen Lindsay, centre, with the St George's hockey team

Anne-Benedicte

Helen Lindsay was the youngest boarder at St George's School in Edinburgh when she started there in 1912. She wrote entries in her Charles Letts' Schoolgirl diaries throughout the war years. From having a cold bath and knitting socks for the soldiers, to learning Latin and being elected prefect, Helen's diaries depict what everyday life was like at the school. She writes of playing cricket and making laughing gas in science, where she adds: "I felt quite cheerful all night, so perhaps it was the effect of that." However, the harrowing glimpses of war are clear, including the day her friend Ethel received word that her brother had been killed, and her own family worries.

5th August 1914
Last night war was declared between Germany and Great Britain. We went along to see Territorials start on cycles to beyond Edinburgh. They got tremendous cheering.

Helen's brother Jack was a second lieutenant in the Black Watch.
23rd November 1916
Mother told me that Jack was wounded. The telegram came from the depot. But she telephoned later to say he was only very slightly wounded.

April 1917
Daddy and mother extracted a piece of bomb half an inch long from Jack's foot. He [Jack] had it since the 13th November. A bomb had burst a yard away. It gave him a slight wound and this piece in the heel, but it is a miracle he wasn't killed.

In March 1918, Jack was reported "missing".
20th March 1918
He may well be a prisoner, but we must wait for news.
12th April 1918
A telegram came at eight o'clock: Jack Lindsay, prisoner, unwounded. Now the awful strain has been relieved and we are all so thankful. I feel I could sing and sing with joy.

Song: The Roses of Picardy – 1917 recording of Eric Pike

Jenny
Marjorie, the eponymous *Patriotic Schoolgirl*, is shown around a war hospital by a cousin who is a VAD, a war time nursing auxiliary:

"In Kitchener Ward the men have mouth organs and tin whistles and combs, and play till you're nearly deafened. We don't like to check them if it keeps up their spirits, poor fellows! You see, there's always such a pathetic side to it. Some of them will be cripples to the end of their days, and they're still so young. It seems dreadful. Think of Peters and Jackson. A man with one leg can't do very much for a living unless he's a clerk, and neither of them is educated enough for that. Their pensions won't be very much. I suppose they'll be taught some kind of handicraft. I hope so, at any rate.'
"Are they all ordinary Tommies here?" asked Marjorie.
"We've no officers. They, of course, are always in a separate hospital. But some of the Tommies are gentlemen, and have been to public schools. There are two over there. We'll go down the other side of the ward and you'll see them. … We must stop and say a word at each bed, or the men will feel left out. We try not to show any favouritism to the gentlemen Tommies."

Betula
Barbara Castle
"Our life during the war then sank into a dull routine. My mother had increasing difficulty in feeding us. The concoction of hers we hated most was a maize pudding which was so distasteful that to get us to eat it she had to bribe us with a spoonful of our severely rationed jam.

The streets were full of men in khaki and my mother did her bit in providing comforts for them. One day she took me with her to the local barracks on some welfare errand and, young though I was, I was conscious of a sad and downbeat atmosphere. The jubilant jingoism of the early war days had gone. So had my father's enthusiasm for the war. He increasingly saw it as the product of competing imperialisms with nothing much to choose between them in their short-sighted folly. The attempt to cloak the horror and waste of war with bursts of '*Land of Hope and Glory*', with its imperial boastfulness, 'Wider still and wider may thy bounds by set: God who made thee mighty make thee mightier yet,' drove him to contempt. I dutifully shocked my friends by refusing to join them in singing it. Love of one's country, my father used to urge, should broaden one's vision, not narrow it. In one of his later articles in the *Bradford Pioneer*, he mused upon this theme. 'The drums beat in our hearts (England, my England) and it is not easy to resist their call, but it is not right for grown men and women to sell the serious interests of humanity for an old song.'

Song: Speedwell by Morfydd Owen (died in 1918) sung by Rosalind
Rosalind
Colston's Girls' School Magazine, Summer 1918
"Early in the Summer Term came Empire Day, which was celebrated this year in no small way. After School Prayers Miss Sparks spoke to us all for a few minutes on the spirit of Empire and the lessons of Empire Day, basing her address upon the message delivered centuries ago by Haggai to the Children of Israel, when they, having returned from captivity to undertake the privilege of re-building the Temple, proved forgetful of their duty, and the prophet was sent to remind them of their responsibilities.

"Miss Sparks showed that the lessons of Duty and Responsibility are still needed, since human nature still remains the same. She reminded us of

England's prosperity since the days of Elizabeth, days when Englishmen first became conscious of the glorious destiny that awaited them, and of the gradual growth, since then, of the Empire of which we are so justly proud; but she also showed how quickly English people had developed the tendency to place too high a value upon such things as wealth and position. In 1914, however, she said, the opportunity came to the nation to prove how high a price Englishmen set upon their *honour*, the struggle which resulted having, as we all know, proved the wealth of love spread over the whole of the Empire.

"But when, Miss Sparks said, this present war had been brought to a satisfactory conclusion, and the time of release had come for us, as for the Israelites of old, the choice would again have to be made between Pleasure and Duty, and loyalty to those who had fought and fallen for us would demand that the latter be chosen.

"… Miss Sparks next spoke more particularly with reference to Empire Day as the *children's* day, seeing that the future of the Empire depends upon her children rather than upon her grown-up sons and daughters…. By the children of to-day, she said, the choice would have to be made between self-pleasing on the one hand and duty or self-sacrifice on the other, the former of which could only produce narrowness and unhappiness of life. West Country children, she added, had a valuable asset in the *willingness* which is so striking a characteristic in them, but this in itself was not enough, - *effort* and *voluntary, active choice* were also necessary if England's future were to prove worthy of the traditions of the past."

Song: *Jerusalem*

What were Schoolgirls Reading in 1918?
Sally Dore

We decided to look at what girls were reading a century before in 2014, to mark the beginning of the First World War. In 1914, of course, the war itself had barely had a chance to impact on reading matter. It seemed like an interesting idea to continue, so it's become a regular feature. In 2016, to tie in with our conference theme of series, I looked more closely at the girls' series that were being written, particularly in the United States. So this time I'm going to take the chance to look at how girls' reading matter reflected the war over the whole period from 1914 to 1918. We know already from Sarah Burns' and Ruth Allen's talks among others how rich a resource girls' fiction can be as an indication of social history in real life, and it also has interesting things to say about the position of girls and women in society, and the aims of writers in writing what they did for their audiences.

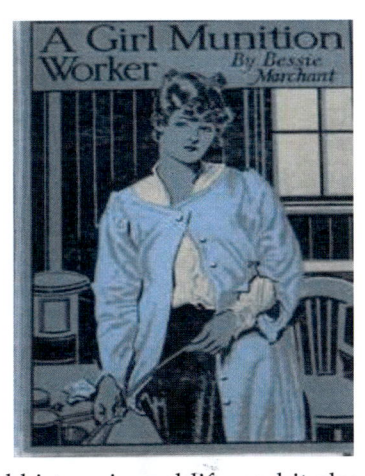

There has not been much study of girls' fiction during World War One. Cadogan and Craig, after their pioneering study of girls' fiction *You're a Brick, Angela*, surveyed it rather superficially in their 1978 book *Women and Children First*, but their review is very broad, *"the experiences of British women and children in the two major wars of the twentieth century, as presented in contemporary and retrospective fiction"*. It is entertaining but rather muddled, both in terms of what they are looking at, social history or literary merit, and chronologically, for example they quote as evidence for wartime attitudes a number of stories that were published after the war. Their assessment is very much of its time both in its view of the First World War and broadly also of girls' fiction (*"the absurd girl characters of Angela Brazil and Bessie Marchant imparted a laughable quality to the genre,"* is one quote from the book), an attitude significantly modified more recently by the work of Rosemary Auchmuty and many other authors. *Over the Top: The Great War and Juvenile Literature in Britain* by Michael Paris (2004) is a much more thorough study. However, it does look at how War is featured in children's reading matter, and as most of the material explicitly referencing war was aimed at boys, what girls were reading gets very much less attention and relies rather too much on Cadogan and Craig. David Budgen's recent book *British Children's Literature and the First World War: Representations since 1914* (2018) looks at children's literature both during the war and in the century since, and uses it as a prism to view changing interpretations of the war itself. He includes a chapter on girls' fiction during the war which is interesting but again cites a limited range of books. Another recent very brief summary by Prof Jean Webb on the *Voices of War and Peace* centenary project surveying children's fiction, while rightly highlighting that not all experiences were reflected in what was written, is hugely generalised and based on a rather limited sample of books girls were reading:

> The attitudes toward warfare in Britain leading up to World War I were deeply rooted in nineteenth-century notions of masculinity embedded in adventure stories for boys and therefore, by polar opposition, in the domestic construction of the feminine. These were the values of the British Empire i.e. endurance, valour, honour, self-sacrifice and patriotism with war tending to be constructed as a great game. Such childhood reading ideologically influenced the men who volunteered to enlist in World War One to protect those values. There were a few books for girls principally by Bessie Marchant which emphasised the 'clichéd' part women played in the war and silenced other aspects of domestic life on the Home Front.

This will also be a necessarily brief survey, but I hope it will highlight some other aspects of what girls were reading during the War, and also indicate how that changed over the course of those years.

At the beginning of the war, as Jean Webb did identify, there was already a strong tradition of adventure books aimed mainly at boys, and this was quickly repurposed to produce stories with the war as a background. To the extent that adventurous literature existed for girls, for example in the books of Bessie Marchant, the same repurposing happened, but it was a much smaller presence to begin with. In the books for boys, the aim, which was undoubtedly explicit in many authors' minds, was to instil the right values to encourage enlisting, since at the beginning of the war the army was composed entirely of volunteers. I should add the caveat, applicable to all that I'm going to discuss, that of course two parties are involved in communication by book – the writer who writes it and the reader who reads it. Whatever a writer's intentions, a reader reads with his or her own education, background and assumptions, and each reading is different; so it is very difficult to generalise about the effect on readers of particular books or genres.

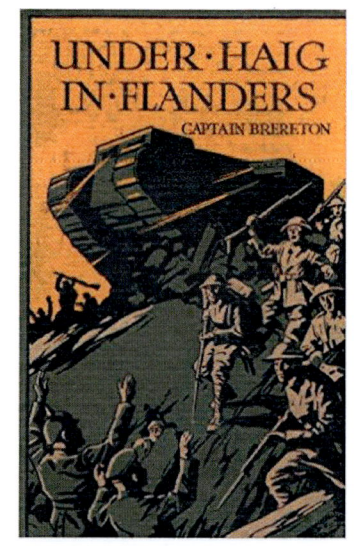

This was the first war with government machinery devoted to propaganda, but at this stage, girls were not seen as targets of propaganda output, as the war was expected to be a quick one on traditional lines and women were not part of the war effort. The *Girls' Own Paper*, always a very conservative organ, cautioned that girls (and indeed their mothers) should "*avoid comic-opera like efforts that involved horses, tents or pseudo-military uniforms*". It seems indubitable, however, that girls were also reading the wartime books aimed at their brothers. Authors in the Henty mould, who had generally used either historical wars or the far-flung corners of the Empire for their adventures, started turning their attention to contemporary situations almost immediately. Captain F.E. Brereton wrote several books which with their subtitles almost create a potted history of the war: in 1915 he produced *Under French's Command: A Story of the Western Front form Neuve Chapelle to Loos*; in 1916, *With Joffre at Verdun; A Story of the Western Front*, *With Our Russian Allies: A Tale of Cossack Fighting in the Eastern Campaign* and *At Grips with the Turk: A Story of the Dardanelles;* in 1917 *On the Road to Baghdad: A Story of Townshend's Gallant Advance on the Tigris* and *Under Haig in Flanders: A Story of Vimy, Messines and Ypres*; in 1918 *The Armoured-Car Scouts: A Tale of the Campaign in the Caucasus*; in 1919 *Under Foch's Command: A Tale of the Americans in France* and *With the Allies to the Rhine: A Story of the Finish of the War*; and in 1920 *With Allenby in Palestine: A Story of the Latest Crusade*. There were plenty of other books not ostensibly aimed at either sex, such as *Great Deeds of the Great War* (1916), by D.A. Mackenzie, which I'm sure girls read too. I will just comment that books aimed at boys were also not a homogeneous mass, and Michael Paris does a good job of tracing the development of what was produced over the course of the war, including the interesting adoption of airmen as heroic quasi-knight figures from the middle of the war onwards.

Over the entire course of the war, of course many books for girls were still published that ignored the war altogether. Among Elsie Oxenham's books, for example, is *A School Camp-Fire* (1917), which doesn't even use the war as what would have been a very plausible reason for Priscilla's father's ill-health. The prolific writer L.T. Meade, wrote a number of books that didn't mention it, such as *The Darling of the School* (1915), *Hollyhock – A Spirit of Mischief* (1916), a family story including the founding of a school, and *The Fairy Godmother* (1917), another school story despite its title. Ju Gosling points out that if writers wished not to refer to the war, the enclosed world of school was one where its exclusion might actually be convincing.

However, as the war developed, fiction written for girls began to integrate the war, and increasingly reflect that fact that for the first time, women were actively involved in the war effort. Jean Webb refers to books emphasising the "clichéd" part played by girls and women in girls' literature of the War (what I might as a shorthand call "knitting and nursing"), but I would argue that it is only in retrospect that it has become clichéd. At the time, the participation to such a great extent of girls and women was new: this was the first war when the "war effort" (expression first used, according to the Oxford English Dictionary, on 23rd December 1914 in the Manchester Guardian) involved a "home front" (expression first used in the Times, 11th April 1917), with everyone subject to a system of "rations" (first used in this sense 29th December 1917) and subject to "air-raids" (expression first used in a book of 1916).

And so what we see are numerous stories that have war as a background to everyday life with detail included to add verisimilitude but no need to explain as readers could be assumed to know what was being referred to from their own experience. Then come books in which the war is impacting on plots and reflecting a more active role played by women in war, both officially, for example in terms of nursing and women's services and munition workers, but also in terms of unofficial adventure for girls, in particular encounters with the enemy (girls trapped behind enemy lines) and with spies at home. Viewing girls' fiction as a whole, we can certainly see that the war was revolutionary in that it genuinely affected virtually everyone in the country: the widespread, almost universal, personal acquaintance with active combatants, the active efforts now required of women on the home front, the presence of refugees, and the new fact of the real physical effect of war on British civilians in terms of air-raids on Britain itself – all find their reflection. And so the depictions of girls' involvement in the war, even in terms of describing everyday life with war as a background, are actually pretty revolutionary in the context of what has come before, and reflect the same huge impact, psychologically as well as physically, that their readers would have been experiencing.

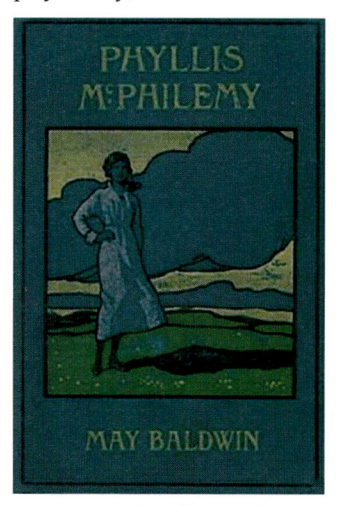

So the first reflection of the War is its impact on everyday life. There are numerous books in which war is a constant background but not a plot-driver. This starts in books published from early in the war such as May Baldwin's ***Phyllis McPhilemy*** (1915), where women's active work perhaps doesn't go much beyond the "nursing and knitting" sphere. Here we see the girls visiting refugees (*"There were Belgian refugees in the small town of Barrow in which the old Priory School was situated, as in most places in England..."*), knitting khaki wool (Phyllis's own shapeless efforts being what she says she'll patent as a "helmoscarfamit", to keep a soldier's head, neck and hands all warm at once!), giving up prizes in favour of certificates so the prize money can be devoted to good causes, and worrying over news, or lack of it, from relations in the forces (Interestingly, we see the headmistress issuing an edict at the beginning of the term that no-one is to abuse the Germans because "*all this abuse and anger against the German nation was very bad for our characters.*" Here May Baldwin, whose outlook had always been very cosmopolitan, was rather different from many other writers of the war years.)

As with fiction aimed at boys, the authors reflect a general attitude that the war effort must be supported and that the cause is right and worthy. But although there was a shared basic assumption in fiction aimed at girls that everyone must play their part and make sacrifices, many authors painted a more nuanced picture, and reflected what must have been the intense worries associated with being at war. In ***The Luckiest Girl in the School*** (1916), by Angela Brazil, Winona is talking to a friend:

"It must be glorious to get letters from the trenches," she said half wistfully one day to Beatrice Howell, who was exulting over a pencil scrawl written by her brother in a dug-out. "I half wish — —"
"No, you don't!" snapped Beatrice. "It's a nightmare to have them in the firing line! Be thankful your brother's still safe at school."

By the end of the war, we see reflected in girls' fiction the fact that the war effort had become distinctly more organised, and that it affected even more facets of everyday life. In Angela Brazil's **For the School Colours**, published in 1918, Silverside School, where more than half the girls are day girls, decides to put on a tea party for crippled children through the "Brave Young Things" Society. Catering is going to prove difficult:

It was utterly impossible for [Miss Thompson, the Principal] to provide a meal for a hundred and thirty children. The Food Controller rationed the school according to the number of its boarders. The Principal was inventive, however, and hit on an excellent solution of the problem. She asked each day girl to bring enough tea, sugar, milk, buns and cake for her own consumption and for half the allowance for one guest, and in this way provided ample for everybody, without anyone being asked to give more than a very small contribution of food.

Angela Brazil's stories were often rather episodic, and a chapter in the middle of **For the School Colours** has the heroine, Avelyn, go off to stay with relations in town, and allows the author to show a multiplicity of the effects of the war on daily life – the chapter is actually called "War Work". Of the five adult children of the family, two sons are in the Flying Corps, one son is in a government ministry, and the two daughters were busy with various kinds of war work.

The Lascelles were very public-spirited people, who were ... anxious to lend a hand in all schemes for the general good. They sewed national costumes for the Serbians, rolled bandages at the War Supply Depot, distributed dinners at the municipal kitchens, taught gymnastic classes at girls' clubs, visited crippled children, got up concerts for wounded soldier, and organized Christmas parties for slum babies. They seemed to be occupied nearly every minutes of the day, and they soon swept Avelyn into the whirl of the war activities. ... She went with Cousin Lilia to the Town Hall, and rather enjoyed standing behind a counter handing out pies, or ladling soup into jugs for the rows of busy people who kept pushing in from the long queue standing in the courtyard outside. She admired the smart quick drill in Mary's gymnasium class, and marvelled that the girls had so much spirit left after their long day's work; she made the whole of a Serbian child's dress herself, with beautiful barbaric red-and-blue trimming on it; she helped to hand cigarettes round to the soldiers at their concert; and she played "Blind Man's Buff" and "Drop the Handkerchief" with the slum children at the New Year's party in the Ragged School.

Two novel institutions due to the war are described at length – and this may well be because at the time she was writing they were fairly new developments that her readers might perhaps not have encountered themselves. Avelyn visits the Crèche where her cousin Gwen volunteers two mornings a week, and discovers that it takes great energy to look after roomfuls of toddlers. "*This day nursery was a new institution in Harlingden, and had been opened in order that women who wished to help at munitions might leave their babies to be taken care of while they were at work.*" And her cousin Mary takes her to see a munitions factory and in particular the hostels provided for the upwards of three thousand new female munition workers, a visit described in considerable detail. Their guide is a friend who is a professionally qualified woman; "*Miss Gordon was doing Government war work in Harlingden. She had taken her certificate for domestic economy at a training college in London, and now held a post in the canteen department of a huge munition factory.*" Brazil explicitly makes the point that [the soldiers'] "*heroism would be of no avail if the hands slacked that forged the weapons at home. The workers who made the munitions, and those who toiled to feed the workers and keep them fit, were taking their share of the burden...*" Here Brazil reflects the far greater involvement of women after four years of war, and the fact that those at home were now thoroughly organised into a true "home front" as part of that war.

British women and girls were also now participants in war in a way in which, living on an island, they had never been before. Because of the development of aerial warfare, Britain was now within reach of direct enemy action, and this touched almost everyone in the country. From December 1914 onwards, raids by Zeppelins and then bomber aircraft became a feature of life, and although the total numbers involved were small, around fourteen hundred people killed and three times that number wounded, widespread press reporting, even though censored, ensured that everyone knew about them. Girls were brought into direct contact with the physical effects of attack; girls' schools were damaged and injuries sustained in, for example, June 1915 in Hull, February 1916 in Broadstairs, and September 1916 in Streatham (the school shown above), and in June 1917 eighteen younger children were killed in a school in Poplar in London. The consequences, air raid drills, air raid shelters and the blackout, affected everyone. This is also reflected in the later fiction of the war, such as E.L. Haverfield's *The Girls of St Olave's* (1919);

Not until about half an hour after the warning had come through did they hear the first dull thuds of distant firing, and knew that the enemy had penetrated the outer defences... It is useless to pretend that a good many who caught that sound did not feel as if their hearts had turned upside down, and some faces became white, some red, some felt their breath coming in uncontrollable little gasps...Even Miss Wilkinson [the Headmistress] turned ashen white when the walls of the house shuddered as if they were shaken by an earthquake, and simultaneously the air was full of the sound of crashing, splintering glass! In that desperate second, no one knew what had happened. What could be going to follow? Had the roof fallen in, and the bricks and mortar crumbled down upon them, no one would have been surprised.

In May Baldwin's **Spoilt Cynthia at School** (1918), sending Cynthia to a school near London is seen as a rash move because of the risk of raids. And indeed, there is a chapter called "The Air-Raid", when damage is done to the house and grounds. The following day the girls all enthusiastically volunteer to help to fill in a crater made by a bomb, while glaziers replace all the school's shattered windows;

"Raid work comes first, Ma'am," said the glazier. "We are not going to let them miserable creatures put us about, and my men will all work overtime and extra hard on a job like this."

Authors also began to exploit the potential for girls and young women to be more actively involved in the war effort. There were two particular unofficial ways in which girls could play an active part which featured as plot devices; catching spies and escaping the enemy in Europe. The number of spies encountered in children's war fiction shows quite extraordinary foresight and organisation on the part of the Germans. Spy scares and catching spies crop up in numerous school and other stories, such as Angela Brazil's **A Patriotic Schoolgirl** (1918). Among the many books featuring girls encountering or escaping from Germans on the Continent, are Bessie Marchant's **Molly Angel's Adventures** (1915), May Baldwin's **Irene to the Rescue** (1916) and Dorothea Moore's **Wanted, An English Girl** (1916), May Wynne's **An English Girl in Serbia** (1916), and **Freda's Great Adventure – A Story of Paris in Wartime** (1917) by Alice Massie.

In terms of official participation in the war, there were also books aimed at girls which featured heroines in their late teens or early 20s, reflecting the new roles open to women. Nursing had been the way in which women previously participated in war, and this was systematised in official nursing services as well as extending to volunteers largely from higher social classes via the Voluntary Aid Detachment (in a similar way that the Territorial Army organised volunteer soldiers). But now women were also participating in other armed services, and these too began to feature in fiction. Thus we have books like Bessie Marchant's *A V.A.D. in Salonika* (1917), and *A Transport Girl in France: The Story of the Adventures of a WAAC* (1919).

Although women had worked in factories before the war, harnessing women's efforts in arenas previously dominated by men such as munitions was also a very noteworthy development in the war, and one that attracted girls' writers as we have seen. Two books in particular stand out. Bessie Marchant published *A Girl Munition Worker* in 1916, with its helpful subtitle *The Story of a Girl's Work during the Great War*. Deborah lives with her crochetty aunt in Canterbury and starts by doing war work (tent-making) three days a week, and substituting for her aunt's cook three days a week so the cook can do war work – without this arrangement the cook would have left altogether to do war work. Her aunt is always making her "*usual plaint of what the war was costing her in daily loss of comfort and prestige*", an attitude contrasted with the much more praiseworthy participation in the war effort of all the younger people. Deborah's brother Bobby's fiancée Gladys is a wealthy orphan.

> *Gladys was working in a cordite factory; she had been there ever since Bobby's regiment had been ordered on active service, and barring accidents, she meant to stay there until he came home again. Her weekly wage went to swell the funds of the Red Cross charities, and she worked as hard as, or harder than, any girl who earned her daily bread.*

Zeppelins and spies both feature, in the course of defeating whom Deborah has to shoot out signalling lights. Gladys does in fact have an accident and has her foot amputated after an explosion at the factory. By the end of the book Deborah is working at the factory, and feels the strain of getting used to being daily in contact with such dangerous material.

Brenda Girvin published ***Munition Mary*** in 1918. This is interesting as it explicitly deals with the prejudice against women working in such occupations. Sir William Harrison, owner of the munitions factory, refuses an interview to would-be journalist Mary Howard;

"He is antagonistic to a girl who has any interest outside her home… He is so opposed to the working-girl that I believe he would ruin himself rather than let one of them set foot inside his workshops."

Mary, born in a generation which is learning the value of women's work, had nothing but impatience for such antiquated views. It was ridiculous, absurd, out-of-date.

Mary later becomes one of the employees at his factory when his nephew Paul persuades him against his better judgement to implement a trial of women workers. Things start going wrong, which seems to vindicate Sir William's viewpoint, but the girls realises it is sabotage, and suspect Sir William himself. Mary, however, plays a key part in unmasking the two clinging womanly women who are actually German spies, at the same time realising that Nephew Paul is the man for her.

Following on all the adventures of that never-to-be forgotten fourth of April it was the climax. All her pluck went. Suddenly she felt she was just a weak girl with no self-control or courage left. She sank down into a chair and burst into a flood of tears.

Two days later Sir William calls while she is making chutney and asks if he can do anything for her. She asks him to give the girls another chance in the factory.

Sir William, eager as he was to grant any request she might make, did not answer until he had fully weighed the matter. This girl had shown intelligence and capability, yet… yet surely nobody could be more feminine than she was. Her tears on that awful night – only a very feminine woman would have given way to tears as she had. Her chutney making! His grandmother had made chutney. She had all the charm of his grandmother. He had been wrong in thinking that when a girl did a man's work she lost her womanliness. He had thought girls could not make shells. Suppose he had been wrong in this too?

There is a strong parallel here with the dilemma facing girls' schools as education for girls became more widely available – how to convey that girls could be intelligent and work hard and play games while still remaining feminine enough to evade serious public criticism.

"To The Officer Commanding"
DORITA FAIRLIE BRUCE

Annuals also tend to be a good reflection of trends in what is being written for children. Taking one at random from 1918, *The Lilac Book for Girls* edited by Mrs Herbert Strang, we can see many of the themes I've touched on above feature in the various stories. Of the twenty-nine in the book, 6 have the war as a prominent element (and another is a stirring account of Anita Garibaldi). An interesting feature is that the tone of these six varies from adventurous to sombre to humorous, perhaps a true indication that war was an ever-present feature against which other activities were played out. *Betty's Bit*, by Florence Bone, is a story about a long-lost relative, framed by the fact of Betty having a brother who is a doctor in the war. *"To the Officer Commanding"* is a spy story by Dorita Fairlie Bruce. Pansy and Peter help a wounded pilot to outwit spies and get important papers to Glasgow, with Peter acting as decoy while Pansy is the real messenger: "*It seems to me one can have plenty of adventures in these days, even if one is only a girl.*" A second story by Dorita Fairlie Bruce, *For Mona's Sake*, is a school story with a background of War; Mona has been killed in a zeppelin raid. *The Spy of Gulls' Nest* by M.E. Gillick appears to be a spy story, although actually the owner of the suspicious cough heard in the secluded gully turns out to be a sheep... *The Longpré Bend* by Margaret Ashworth is a war story set in France, where three French children outwit the Germans to uncover some spies and Marcelle, the girl, heroically shoots some rapids in order to deliver important papers. Finally *Jack V.A.D.* by Esmee Rhoades gives us glimpses of the home front.

It is a horrid feeling to wake up one morning and think that you are neither useful nor ornamental. And when this happens for many mornings, it becomes unbearable. In our family, everybody of a "do-able" age was doing something. That is, everybody except me. Mother was mixed up with all sorts of Societies; Father "interpreted" and "censored." Philip was fighting "Somewhere in France." Ronnie made bits of shells in the workshop at School..., Mab knitted comforters and things beautifully, while Kenneth was the only "slacker" (the privilege of extreme youth), with the exception of my stupid self.

Just when I was feeling a drone in the hive, a useless encumbrance, and a miserable person, a sudden announcement by Mother raised my dropping spirits.

"Mrs Ballister is forming a Voluntary aid Class to teach Home-Nursing and First-Aid Treatment," she observed one afternoon, while pouring the tea. "She mentioned you as a 'possible'."

"Oh, Mother! I'd love it," was my delighted response. "Do you think I should be of any use?"

"There is no reason why you shouldn't try, Jack," she answered, diplomatically.

Perhaps needless to say, after practising on various members of the family, Jack happens to be present when a recuperating VC is thrown from his motorbike and severs an artery, and manages to save his life with her now-effective bandages, and receives effusive thanks from his hitherto aloof mother. (See the illustration here, surprisingly lacking in blood – perhaps because the tone of the story is humorous?)

It is very clear from the fiction aimed at girls that many authors considered the war had allowed girls and women new opportunities, and had proved that they could rise to the challenges. Angela Brazil is one who voices this frequently, for example here in ***The Madcap of the School*** (1917):

"…I think the war will have made a great difference to many of our men."

"And to our women too, I hope," said Miss Beasley [the headmistress], who, unnoticed by Veronica, had joined the group. "It would be a poor thing for the country if only the men came purified out of this time of trouble. 'A nation rises no higher than its women!' And now is Woman's great opportunity. I think she is taking it. She is showing by her work in hospitals, in canteens, on the land, in offices, or in public service, how she can put her shoulder to the wheel and help in her country's hour of need. I believe this war will have broken down many foolish old traditions and customs, and that people will be ready afterwards to live more simple, natural lives than they did before. The school-girls of to-day are the women of to-morrow, and it is on you that the nation will rely in years to come. Don't ever forget that! Try to prove it practically!"

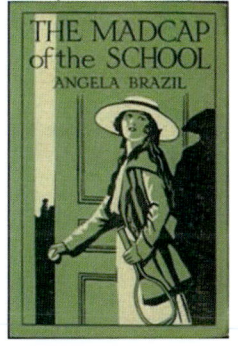

This was perhaps the prevailing view voiced in girls' fiction by the end of the war, that the position of women had clearly changed, that women had proved themselves and opportunities had opened up. But as the war ended in 1918, did writers – and readers – expect attitudes and opportunities to return to the pre-war status quo, or to continue to develop?

Budgen, David; *British Children's Literature and the First World War: Representations since 1914* (2018)
Cadogan, M, and Craig, P; *Women and Children First* (1978)
Gosling, Ju; *Virtual Worlds of Girls*; http://www.ju90.co.uk/indexful.htm
Paris, Michael; *Over the Top: The Great War & Juvenile Literature in Britain* (2004)
Webb, Jean; *The Silenced War*; https://www.voicesofwarandpeace.org/portfolio/the-silenced-war/

Baldwin, May; *Phyllis McPhilemy* (1915), *Irene to the Rescue* (1916), *Spoilt Cynthia at School* (1918)
Brazil, Angela; *The Luckiest Girl in the School* (1916), *The Madcap of the School* (1917), *For the School Colours* (1918), *A Patriotic Schoolgirl* (1918)
Girvin, Brenda; *Munition Mary* (1918)
Haverfield, E.L.; *The Girls of St Olave's* (1919)
Marchant, Bessie; *Molly Angel's Adventures* (1915), *A Girl Munition Worker* (1916), *A VAD in Salonika* (1917), *A Transport Girl in France: The Story of the Adventures of a WAAC* (1919).
Massie, Alice; *Freda's Great Adventure – A Story of Paris in Wartime* (1917)
Meade, L.T.; *The Darling of the School* (1915), *Hollyhock – A Spirit of Mischief* (1916), *The Fairy Godmother* (1917)
Moore, Dorothea; *Wanted, An English Girl* (1916)
Oxenham, Elsie J.; *A School Campfire* (1917)
Strang, Mrs Herbert (ed); *The Lilac Book for Girls* (1918)
Wynne, May; *An English Girl in Serbia* (1916)

Me, Louise Plewes and the Anne Digby Mystery
Louise Plewes

I've chosen to look at Anne Digby partly because these books are "my era", and also because it didn't look like anyone else had done it already! Firstly I'm going to cover what we know about the author and her route to becoming a writer. Then I'll go on to look at her books, mainly focussing on the *Trebizon* series, but also the other series (and non-series) books she wrote, and her books for younger children. I'll discuss some similarities and differences between the *Trebizon* series and her other books. On *Trebizon* I'll talk about the key themes running through the books, my favourite *Trebizon* moments, and unanswered questions in the series.

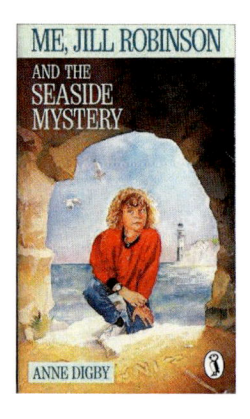

The Author

So, what do we know about Anne? Actually I found it very difficult to find out much about her. The main sources that I used are: *The Encyclopaedia of Girls School Stories* by Sue Sims and Hilary Clare; an interview which Hilary Clare did with Anne Digby in 1994 in FOLLY magazine; and the blurb at the start of the Fidra edition of *Fifth Year Friendships at Trebizon* from 2008.

And then last week, I stumbled across her comic serials and picture strip stories. Last month there was the International Graphic Novel and Comic Convention in Bournemouth and Anne was pictured being interviewed.

Anne was born in either 1935 or 1942 in Kingston-upon-Thames and is still alive and well, and has a Twitter account. Anne Digby is a pseudonym - her real name is Pat Davidson. But I am going to refer to her as Anne. Anne attended North London Collegiate School (a private day school for girls), then worked as a magazine journalist, press officer for Oxfam and lived in Paris at one stage. She is married to a writer, has 4 grown up children, grandchildren, and lives in Sussex.

Anne had always wanted to write books. In primary school she won a hardback book [*Sheila's Glorious Holiday*] in a poetry competition and the poem was published in a children's magazine. She also wrote and drew for an unofficial school magazine a bit like Rebecca Mason and the Juniper Journal. Aged 16, Anne became an editorial trainee in London, working on *School Friend* and during the 1960s and early 1970s she wrote both stories and picture scripts for *School Friend, Girl,* and *Tammy*. She also wrote *Ella's Big Sacrifice*, a full length book published by *Schoolgirl's Own Library* in 1960, and some horse and other sporty stories such as *Olympia Jones* and *Tennis Star Tina*. Her journalism training taught her tight plotting, cliffhanger endings to chapters and thinking the story through visually. And I think this is very evident in the length and style of the Trebizon books.

Interestingly, in the late 1970s Anne published in both comic and book formats so *A Horse Called September* began as a picture strip serial, was spotted by a publisher and turned into her first full-length book in 1976 and then *First term at Trebizon* which came out first as a full length book was adapted into a picture strip serial.

The *Trebizon* books were written partly for wish-fulfilment, using traditional elements from her own schooldays, and partly from the experiences of her children and their friends. Anne wanted to write a modern, contemporary boarding school series with a small, self-contained world, giving scope for adventures. This was against the trend in publishing at the time for "issues" books, gritty reality etc, but the series has been surprisingly popular and is still in print today in modern colourful editions and as e-books, so she must have been doing something right! Surprisingly, she says she only ever read one school story book *The Girl Who Was Expelled* by A M Irvine and found it "gloomy".

The Books

Anne is best known for the Trebizon series, but she also wrote the following other titles:

- Her first book *A Horse Called September* was published 42 years ago in 1976, and followed by *A Quicksilver Horse* in 1979 and *The Big Swim of the Summer* (1979, school/sport).
- In the 1980s she published books on *Ghostbusters*, *Indiana Jones* and *Roland Rat*. As you do. (I've slipped this reference in to check if anyone is still awake…)
- The *Me, Jill Robinson* series, 6 titles published 1983-1985. Obviously this is the series I took my talk title inspiration from.
- The *Jug Valley Juniors* series of 6 books published in 1992-1993.
- The *Three R's Detectives* series of 3 books published 1991-1995.
- Most recently, the 6 continuations of Enid Blyton's *Naughtiest Girl* series 1999/2000.

What do any of these have in common with the Trebizon series?

- The two pony books - nothing, but these are very good, like K M Peyton.

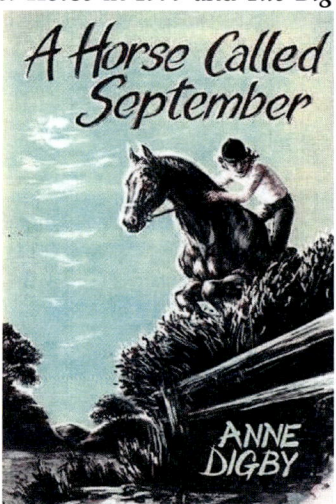

- *The Big Swim of the Summer* is a school book, about friendships and rivalry, and about sport - she writes well about sport. A little bit like Peyton's *Who, Sir? Me, Sir?* but without the humour.
- *Me, Jill Robinson*; Jill is not Rebecca, she is younger and goes to mixed, state school. But the mystery element is similar.
- *Jug Valley Juniors* and *Three Rs Detectives* are mixed, state schools, for younger children, school/mystery/adventure books.
- And then back to the school story genre with the *Naughtiest Girl* continuations.

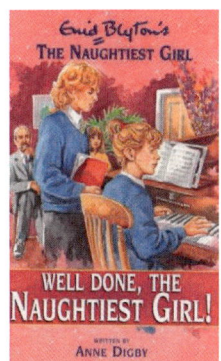

The Trebizon Series

And so finally onto the *Trebizon* series. These books were actually written between 1978 and 1994, sixteen actual years covering 4 fictional years from the second to the fifth forms of secondary school. They are set when they were written, so we have 70s fashions mentioned in the early books, but denim jackets, walkmans, and GCSE coursework by the end of the series.

There were also several publishers, stops and starts in the series.

All the books were first published in hardback (presumably for libraries), I don't have any in hardback. These were followed by paperback editions, with three cover styles: i) the original red and white to match the hardback, ii) the Puffin editions and iii) the modern editions by Egmont. The last few titles were incredibly hard to find a few years back before they were republished by Fidra. The whole series is now also available as e-books. In my research I also came across several omnibus editions, and a CD version of *First Term* which Leeds Library have not yet discarded. I also found German translations with amusing titles such "Always trouble with boys" and "A nice summer".

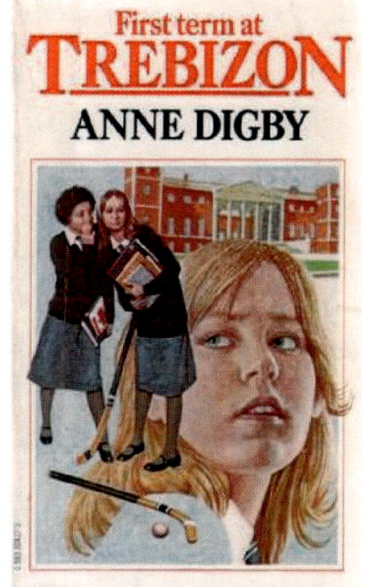

The books didn't come across to me as dated, even though I was 2 in 1978 when the first book was written/set, and 18 and doing my A levels in 1994 when the final one came out. Yes, the 1990s were different from the 1970s, but not as different as the 2010s are from the 1990s, no internet, no mobile phones...but these books are still in libraries today with the bright new covers.

It puzzles me that the books are so short, barely 120 pages, about a 45 minute read. Who are the books aimed at? A bright 7 year old can cope with a book that length, but the content is too advanced for them. It's almost as though the 3 separate, slim books covering a single academic year should have been one volume.

Key Themes in the *Trebizon* Books

The main character in the series is Rebecca Mason. She starts at Trebizon School, a girls' boarding school in the West Country, in the Second Year. She previously attended a state school in London, but is coming to Trebizon because her Dad will be working in Saudi Arabia and the firm is paying her fees. At first Rebecca struggles to make friends. Eventually she find her place as part of "the six" as they are called: Tish (Ishbel) Anderson, and Sue Murdoch, as well as Sally Elphinstone (Elf), Mara Leonodis, and Margot Lawrence. And so together they work their way up the school.

What kind of heroine is Rebecca? She's pretty typical. She's good at English, Literature, Languages, and History, she wants to write for the school magazine. So far, so Joey Bettany. But she's also sporty, good at hockey, running, ice skating, but most of she is a talented tennis player. And it's this growing conflict between her academic potential and her tennis career that runs through the later books.

The books also feature boys. Generally nice sensible boys who are the brothers of other girls at the school. The boys study at Garth College nearby and there are plenty of matches to cheer at, end of year dances to attend, going out for coffee and cake etc. It's all pretty innocent. Then there's the mystery solving element. In most, if not all, the books there is a problem to be solved and the six turn into "action committee" and off they go, looking for clues and solving the puzzle.

My Trebizon Top Three

I said I would talk about my favourite Trebizon moments: the poem, the maths exam and tennis. I wasn't at all obsessed with beaches, surfing or the cool shade of a green tree when I wrote this talk in the heat wave this week...

<u>The poem</u>

I love the moment in the first book when baddy Elizabeth Exton who has stolen Rebecca's half-finished poem and published it under her own name in the school magazine is summoned in front of Miss Wellbeck, the headmistresss, to explain herself. Rebecca shows that in fact she and not Elizabeth was the true author of the poem by knowing that she had borrowed the first line "There's a certain slant of light on winter afternoons..." from an Emily Dickinson poem and then added her own poem on from that point. Elizabeth does not know the Emily Dickinson line and is exposed as a thief and a liar (and expelled).

The maths exam
Maths is never popular in school story books. I don't know why, I'm a STEM ambassador for schools and I do maths for a living. Anyway, Rebecca's not bad at maths, she's just got weaknesses as she's not familiar with the syllabus and methods used at Trebizon. But the maths exam gets all out of proportion because, at the end of the Second Year, a) your exam results in the year-end exam and b) the letter your surname starts with, together determine which of the school Houses you will go to live in for the rest of your time up to and including GCSEs (Sixth Form is a different house). Basically, Rebecca has struggled with maths all term and the new young dishy maths teacher has ignored her. With coaching from her friends, she has improved, but when the exam results are announced, her maths grade isn't up to scratch. So Rebecca will be in another house, away from her friends. But the ink on the paper is smudged; is there some sort of mystery here....?

Tennis
And my third favourite moment is the painting that Rebecca's Sixth Form heroine Pippa paints of Rebecca in *Tennis Term*, relaxed against the trunk of the old cedar tree on a beautiful summer's day, having just won the tennis cup. Pippa gives it to Rebecca as a gift. And here it is on the cover. That's how I imagine her looking. It's just a lovely illustration.

Trebizon – the Unanswered Questions
The series ended in 1994 with the publication of the final title *The Unforgettable Fifth at Trebizon*. But (perhaps deliberately?) it leaves so many unanswered questions...will Rebecca choose Tennis over University, Cliff over Robbie, will her GCSE grades be enough to get her into Sixth Form? I'm sure these are the questions most fans would like Anne to clear up. I did stumble across some fan fiction continuations....but that's another story…

Sources
FOLLY 13 1994; Interview with Anne Digby by Hilary Clare, pages 38-39.

The blurb at the start of FIDRA 2008 edition of *Fifth Form Friendships at Trebizon*.

The Encyclopaedia of Girls School Stories, Sue Sims and Hilary Clare 2000, Ashgate.

https://jintycomic.wordpress.com/2016/01/15/anne-digby-interview/

http://www.booksmonthly.co.uk/tammy.html

http://interviewswithwriters.com/interview-with-author-anne-digby/

https://jintycomic.wordpress.com/tag/first-term-at-trebizon/

Bibliography
The Trebizon Series
First Term at Trebizon (1978), WH Allen
Second Term at Trebizon (1979) WH Allen
Summer Term at Trebizon (1979) WH Allen
Boy Trouble at Trebizon (1980) Granada, Illus Gavin Rowe
More Trouble at Trebizon (1981) Granada, Illus Gavin Rowe
The Tennis Term at Trebizon (1981) Granada, Illus Gavin Rowe

Summer Camp at Trebizon (1982) Granada, Illus Gavin Rowe
Into the Fourth at Trebizon (1982) Granada, Illus Gavin Rowe
The Hockey Term at Trebizon (1984) Granada
Fourth Year Triumphs at Trebizon (1985) Granada
The Ghostly Term at Trebizon (1990) Swift Books
Fifth Year Friendships at Trebizon (1991) Swift Books
Secret Letters at Trebizon (1993) Straw Hat
The Unforgettable Fifth at Trebizon (1994) Straw Hat

Me, Jill Robinson Series
Me, Jill Robinson and the TV Quiz (1983)
... and the Seaside Mystery (1983)
... and the Christmas Panto (1983)
... and the School Camp Adventure (1984)
... and the Perdou Painting (1984)
... and the Stepping Stones Mystery (1985)

Jug Valley Juniors (1992 & 1993)
The Photofit Mystery at Jug Valley Juniors
Boys versus Girls at Jug Valley Juniors
The Headmaster's Ghost at Jug Valley Juniors
Hands up at Jug Valley Juniors
The Magic Man at Jug Valley Juniors
Poison Pen at Jug Valley Juniors

Naughtiest Girl [Blyton] Hodder
The Naughtiest Girl Keeps a Secret (1999)
The Naughtiest Girl Helps a Friend (1999)
The Naughtiest Girl Saves the Day, (1999)
Well Done, The Naughtiest Girl! (1999)
The Naughtiest Girl Wants to Win (2000)
The Naughtiest Girl Marches On (2000)

Three Rs Detectives series
Three R Detectives and the milk bottles mystery (1991)
Mystery of the missing footprints (1992)
Three R Detectives and the silly postman mystery (1995)

Other (non series books)
A Horse Called September (1976)
Quicksilver Horse (1979)
The Big Swim of the Summer (1979)

Other children's books
Ghostbusters (1984)
Roland Rat (1987)
Indiana Jones (1989)

Clare Mallory: The Person behind the Pseudonym
Barbara Robertson

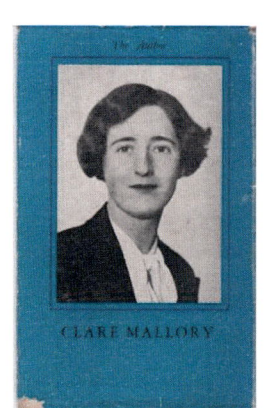

To introduce myself: I am a New Zealander, current editor of *The Abbey Gatehouse*. I wrote introductions to GGBP editions of **Pen and Pencil Girls, Juliet Overseas** and **League of the Smallest**.

I tried in the brief synopses in the bibliography below to highlight some of the themes of her books. She started writing them in wartime. But, as I am about to show you, this was not the start of her writing career. Her school stories, while appearing to be typical school stories, set in boarding schools, like Enid Blyton whose *Malory Towers* series encompassed 1946 to 1951 and *St Clare's* 1941 to 1945, were nevertheless much better written in terms of language, character, situations, complexity, humour, etc. Amongst aficionados of School Stories, she frequently ranks amongst the top four, some even ranking her above writers with a more extensive series of stories, like Elsie Oxenham and Elinor Brent-Dyer.

98

However, this talk is going to be about the person who wrote as Clare Mallory, rather than about her books. Those of you who know the books well should be able to see from her life where some of the themes or episodes in the books came from.

Having said that, I wish to begin by referring to the review of *Merry Begins* that was printed in The NZ Listener in 24 October 1947.

Book Review
New Zealand Listener 24 October 1947.
GIRLS AT SCHOOL
MERRY BEGINS *by Clare Mallory.*
Geoffrey Cumberlege, for the Oxford University Press.
Clare Mallory was lucky in getting the Oxford University Press to take her book – a boarding school story set in New Zealand about supposedly New Zealand girls. The school is in Dunedin (where the sun always shines more often than not), Auckland and Wellington are mentioned, there is a visit to a sheep station in Canterbury (sheep aren't mentioned), and the school year starts in February. But that is about all there is of New Zealand in it. There is the familiar plot of the unpopular prefect Winning Through with the help of the new girl. But there are far too many House points, too much House pride and House Honour. When perhaps eighty per cent of New Zealand children attend day and mixed high schools, it is unfortunate that overseas readers are receiving such a strange impression of the school life of our girls. Clare Mallory can write, but I would like to see her talents used in a school story that will be about the kind of school you and I went to, and about children like the kids down the street.
D.R.

And contrast that with the start of the section on Clare Mallory in *A Sea Change – 145 Years of New Zealand Junior Fiction* by Betty Gilderdale, which was printed in 1982.

> *The most prolific writer of New Zealand school stories is Clare Mallory. Her eight books were published between 1947 and 1951, and are all good examples of their kind. They not only have the expected ingredients, but go further to explore the nature of authority and its place in the school system. Several of the books have as their central character a girl who questions the disciplines imposed by staff and prefects and who has to come to terms with the reasons for her rebellion. The underlying theme of the books is summarised by the headmistress of Tremayne School when she has cause to reprimand one of the characters in Merry Again: "Rebels sometimes do great good in the world. But people who rebel against the rules for their own selfish ends do good to no one; they are even most unkind to themselves. You are at Tremayne's to learn, not*

only French and Science. What you need to learn most is how to discipline yourself."

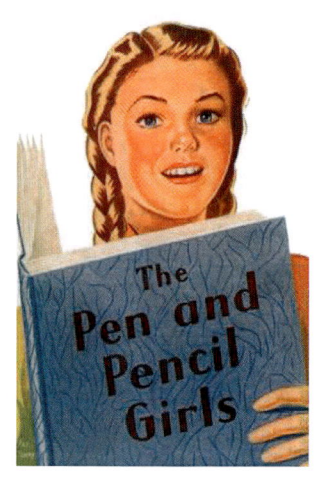

Clare Mallory wrote of the world she knew – the advice given to young would-be-writers in *Pen and Pencil Girls*. In the 1940s, Oxford would be unlikely to be interested in the New Zealand 'kids down the street', and New Zealand private schools **were** on the English model and like Tremayne's. Even when I went to Wellington Girls' College in 1954 we had Prefects and Houses (though mainly for Sports). And even now NZ private schools and many State Schools have Houses and Prefects.

Winifred Constance McQuilkan (later Hall) was born in Invercargill in September 1913. Some sources say the 25th September and the researcher Rex Johnson (who wrote the Introduction to the GGBP reprint of *The New House at Winwood*) says that her birth certificate gives 4th September.

Much of my information about the life of this author comes from her life-long friend, Janet Maconie, whom I first met in the early 1990s. (Hilary Clare corresponded with Janet when writing about Clare Mallory for *The Encyclopaedia of Girls' School Stories*.) Janet and Winnie first met in 1924 when they were both, as 10 ½ year olds, in standard 5 (Form 1 or Year 7, in today's terminology) at school in Invercargill in the deep south of New Zealand. Winnie and Janet loved school stories, especially the 'classic' Cliff House stories in *School Friend* magazine. (Just as the girls in *Pen and Pencil Girls* loved reading *Schoolgirl's Herald* and *The School Chum*.) They read widely and loved writing their own stories, contributing to the Invercargill Competitions in the School Holidays as well as to the "Little Southlanders" page in the Southland Times.

This experience is used in *Pen and Pencil Girls*, which is the most autobiographical of her books. And on page 155 (1st ed), page 161(GGBP) the Pen and Pencil Girls are told to *'go down to your newspaper offices and glance at back files.'* So in 2009, I regularly spent time in the Newspapers section of the National Library hunting through their microfilms of *The Southland Times* of the 1920s for contributions by Winnie McQuilkan, and copying them onto a memory stick. Here is one contribution.

Southland Times, Saturday 6 March 1926
Competitions (59th Test)

For Cousins 14 years and under. Poem on "The Streamlet".
Highly Commended: Cousin Winnie McQuilkan (12).

So still and beautiful it gleams, in brown-eyed tenderness,
   A tiny fairy streamlet all a-fringed with maiden-hair.
No poet could define the charm it holds in its caress,
   But peace beyond all earthly thought is softly centred there.
On either side there seems to be just miles of waving grasses
   Rustling when the winds blow, but quiet when they are still.
There's clover on the gentle breath of every breeze that passes,
   And 'neath their quiet touches, the stream remains so still.
And oh, the gentle water seems to me to be enchanted
   When the sun reaches the hillside and tips it with gold
That "Oberon," the fairy king, to the sunset fay has granted
   To scatter round right everywhere, o'er streamlet, hill and wold.
And it lies all enchanted with these spells of fairy weather,
   And the dainty little stream-elves one expects to see like this,
Are laughing and a-dancing in my streamlet all together,
   So isn't this the height of perfect bliss.
   -- 2 marks to Cousin Winnie McQuilkan (12), 255 Yarrow Street, Invercargill.

And some of the comments from "Cousin Betty":

Cousin Winnie McQuilkan is sending me the best poem she has done, yet has just missed making of it a very fine piece of work indeed. I like the way she starts off – the phrase "brown-eyed tenderness"; but I do not like the lazy sign betrayed in "a-fringed" – this 'a' before parts of verbs is, in the first place, an archaic use, and secondly, it does not enhance the value of a word in any degree. . . Then, Winnie, you have used "still" to rhyme with "still" – shocking! . . . The poem, on the whole, pleases me because of the originality in it, and the things attempted in it, which makes it an ambitious effort. I want Winnie to act on my advice, and I think the next verse she sends me will be a very great improvement on this already promising start.

   Winnie's mother died during her third form year at Southland Girls' High School. For the next 9 years she lived in private board, spending holidays with an aunt's family or with friends. Hence her teenage years were **not** spent with the 'kids down the street', the phrase used in the Listener review. Winnie was dux of Southland Girls' High School and won a university entrance Scholarship which took her to Otago University. Janet says: "*She was probably the brightest woman student of her year*". While at Otago, she wrote a column for the University newspaper '*The Critic*' under the name of Susan Schnozzletippet.

Here is the start on her column published on Thursday, June 8th, 1933.
SIMPLE SUSIE SMITES HER SEX.

I am just a simple little girl from the country and I feel dreadfully insignificant in this big city especially when I attend my lectures at the wonderful University here and find the students so smart, and the night life of the place, so my landlady says, is something frightful, but who are we to judge others. Anyway, that's what I always think. And you know the language is so queer; for instance, when I say smart I mean clever, but people here use words with quite different meanings, it's so confusing. Someone said to me about a girl in French III, My dear, she's utterly dumb. And I said, poor thing, how does she get on with oral? And the other lady said, Aren't you a sap? And the only sap I know is out of trees, or verb sap, which is what Father says when he wants to be sententious.

[This is the first paragraph and is about one tenth of the whole article.]

In 1935 she graduated with an MA (Hons) in English and Classics. The Classics were her greatest love as shown by the poems with which she won the Macmillan Brown Prize in 1935 and again in 1937, by which time she was a member of the staff at St Hilda's Collegiate School. [The Macmillan Brown Prize, for excellence of English composition in verse or prose, was initially offered to students of the University of Otago, but was later offered to all undergraduates in New Zealand and graduates of up to three years' standing.]

I have copies of parts of both of these, thanks to Bettina Vine (who is with us today). The 1935 one is very Classical and very long; and not always easy to understand. The shorter 1937 poem is addressed to "American and British motion picture corporations", and is written as if by "Marcus Tullius Cicero" who sends "cordial salutations" to his readers. Here is the start of the second poem:

THE PASSION FOR IMMORTALITY
To American and British motion picture corporations
From Marcus Tullius Cicero come cordial salutations.

My friends, we who address you here ourself have been of late

A pillar of society, the saviour of a State;
Philosopher and poet, too; the mouthpiece of legality;
So now, returned to earth a space, from Stygian depths reprieved,
We find the truth that greets our eyes can scarcely be believed!
For films of Roman times are shown, of dubious authenticity.
But what is worse, we, Cicero, get none of the publicity!
Instead – O shame! O infamy! (We must speak with asperity,
So lacerated are we at our treatment by posterity.)
Instead – are we not justified in being acrimonious?
The screen perpetuates the name of vile M. Antonius!
[And so on, for another 48 lines.]

Winnie then spent two years in Oxford at Somerville College on a post-graduate scholarship, returning with a BA (Hons). In 1942, at the young age of 28, Winnie was appointed Principal of Columba College, a private girls' school in Dunedin. This became her first real home since childhood. In 1995 I interviewed a middle-aged woman who had been at Columba College during Winifred McQuilkan's time as Headmistress. The girls called her Quills – a reference to her name and also to her love of English writing. I wrote an article for FOLLY (July 1996) giving a pupil's view of their young Headmistress. Here are a few of those comments:

Quills was attractive in appearance. She was little, short and plumpish, with dark hair and pink and white skin. . . She was interested in fashion, wore nice clothes and enjoyed dressing. She had a good reading voice and the girls enjoyed being read to. She was careful about accents, encouraged standard Oxford English, and discouraged New Zealand/Australian twang. . . She was a marvellous English teacher, especially to someone who enjoyed literature. . . She was her own person and had her own personality. For instance, when asked why she wrote schoolgirl stories, she said that "only school stories and detective stories paid." . . . As a headmistress, in many ways, Quills was very liberal. For instance, she allowed Seventeen magazine and Gone with the Wind in the school library, which her successor quickly had removed. Boarders were allowed to go out to private dances, if she knew the parents hosting them. . . . She usually charmed parents and Board members, and had a knack of getting her own way with them. She had that important talent of being friendly and being able to present herself and her ideas well. . . . Hockey was important and strong in the school, as in all Dunedin schools in those days [and as in many of her books]. . . . Quills was a good cook and encouraged this domestic art because it was creative. Otherwise her sympathies were more with academic learning. . . . Possibly the best summing of an ex-pupil's reaction is that Quills is remembered fondly with a smile.

People whose mothers went to Columba have said that the *Merry* books are true to life. And Bettina Vine, who was a pupil at Columba many years later, says in her Introduction to the GGBP reprints of the *Merry* books: '*Even though Merry started Form Three nearly forty years before I did, the school is presented so realistically that I found it quite bizarre to see so much of my school life in print.*'

Readers of the *Merry* books are no doubt aware of how these came to be written. During and after WWII, schools in New Zealand were encouraged to send food parcels to schools in Britain, especially milk products, honey, fruitcakes and even lard or cleaned dripping. These mainly tinned items had to be sewn into hessian bags with cloth outer coverings, and to entertain the girls of Columba College while doing this tedious task, their headmistress would read to them. But there was difficulty finding a story that all of the girls had not already read, so she made up stories about girls in a school similar to their own. Though she did not use the names of her girls, many of the characters were recognisable as being based on pupils they knew.

Share your food

WITH A HUNGRY BOY OR GIRL IN BRITAIN . . .

You know how much the boys and girls in Great Britain need extra food. Under the Schools Gift Food scheme you simply bring packets or tins of food to school. It is all packed together and sent to a school in Britain. Tell mum and dad all about it and ask them to help.

SOME OF THE FOODS TO SEND:

Powdered Milk (full cream), Condensed Milk (full cream; sweetened if possible). Canned Cheese. Dried Fruit. Fruit Cakes (in tins). Tinned Meats. Treacle and Golden Syrup (carefully sealed). Honey and Jam (in tins). Lard or Cleared Dripping (in tins). Malted Milk. Chocolate.

SEND SCHOOL PARCELS TO BRITAIN

Share your Food advertisement from **Conquest** *magazine* 1947

[As an aside, recently we found in a 1948 *Collins Magazine for Boys and Girls*, an advertisement for a competition where you could win "Free Food from Canada every month for a year" by persuading your friends to become subscribers to Collins Magazine for Boys and Girls!]

Her friend and secretary, Marjory Taverner (see dedication to *Merry Again*) suggested *Merry Begins* could be published, typed up the manuscript and sent it to Oxford University Press, who readily accepted it and the next two books, publishing all three books in 1947. OUP sent a review copy of *Merry Begins* to the New Zealand Listener, who sent it on to the National

Library Service. But it was then reviewed not by the experienced head librarian but by a student who was working with her. At that time all reviews were credited only with initials, not full names, so other librarians reading the review assumed it to carry the weight and reputation of the head librarian. Janet told me that Winnie always maintained that this review 'killed my book' as public libraries would not stock it, believing that they could take the word of the National Library Service.

In *Columba College: The First Fifty Years 1915 – 1965*, is the following brief biography giving a summary of her time at the school.

Biography of Principal, Columba College

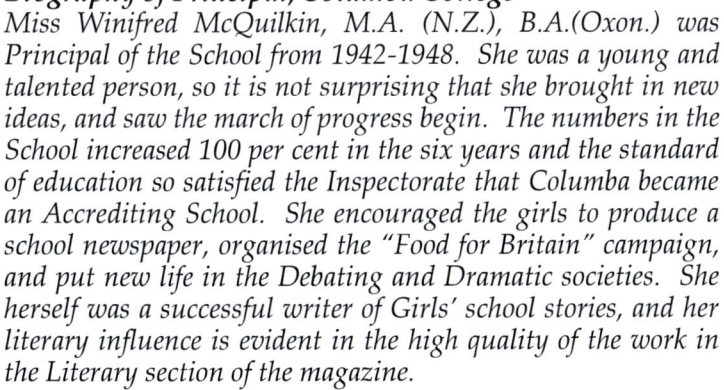

Miss Winifred McQuilkin, M.A. (N.Z.), B.A.(Oxon.) was Principal of the School from 1942-1948. She was a young and talented person, so it is not surprising that she brought in new ideas, and saw the march of progress begin. The numbers in the School increased 100 per cent in the six years and the standard of education so satisfied the Inspectorate that Columba became an Accrediting School. She encouraged the girls to produce a school newspaper, organised the "Food for Britain" campaign, and put new life in the Debating and Dramatic societies. She herself was a successful writer of Girls' school stories, and her literary influence is evident in the high quality of the work in the Literary section of the magazine.

At the end of 1948, Winnie left Columba College to marry Frank Hall, whom she had met at University where he was studying medicine, and they left New Zealand for England where Frank was to continue his studies. They spent three and a half years in Britain. During this time Winnie continued writing, including giving talks on the BBC on Children's books and authors. She also attended many plays and films and travelled extensively in Europe. In 1951 they had a baby son, Francis, who lived for only six hours.

Amongst her writings at this time was a critical account of girls' school stories and their authors. (Perhaps the text of the BBC talks?) Janet Maconie told me that this had not been submitted to a publisher because another book on school story writers had just been published and Winnie thought no one would be interested in her manuscript. The book that seems to fit this description/situation is *Tales out of School* by Geoffrey Trease which was published in 1949. Unfortunately the manuscript of Winnie's book only exists as Chapters 3 to 16. It is held in the Alexander Turnbull Library in Wellington.

Back in NZ she taught briefly at Wellington Girls' College, and Samuel Marsden Collegiate, before tutoring in English at Victoria University of Wellington. Recently I discovered that a friend we have known through The Arthur Ransome Society was taught Latin by "Mrs Hall" at WGC in the fifth form. Here is what she says:

Officially of course she was Mrs Hall, but we referred to her among ourselves as Winnie. She swept into our classroom, short, plumpish, and energetic. In those days teachers at College wore their academic gowns while teaching. We knew the difference between master's and bachelor's gowns. Most of the teachers had bachelor's degrees, so Winnie's master's gown gave her immediate status in our eyes. She had a bit of an educated/BBC-sort of English accent, and I think we knew she had come from England, so it was a surprise to me to learn, only a few years ago, that she was a New Zealander.

Winnie seemed to assume a greater degree of engagement on our part than most of the other teachers. She expected and gently demanded response and interaction from us as a group, where other teachers often seemed to regard us more as sponges for the information they were providing. She was enthusiastic about her subject, and often told us extra bits of information which made it more interesting. She was always in charge of a lesson, and in control of the class, and although she would answer spontaneous questions that had minimal connection with our work, she could not be side-tracked.

Winnie retired from Victoria at the end of 1978. Frank died in March 1979. Winnie's own health deteriorated and in 1986 she was permanently hospitalised with Alzheimer's and died on 20 April 1991.

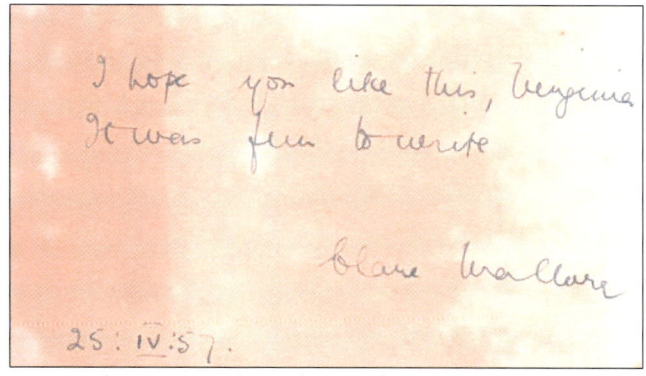

My copy of **Tony Against the Prefects** has an inscription with her signature. *"I hope you like this, Virginia. It was fun to write."*

Clare Mallory's Books

Clare Mallory published 10 books with OUP during her lifetime, between 1947 and 1951. Eight were school stories, while two were about school-age girls and their life outside school. The two previously unpublished manuscripts held in the Alexander Turnbull Library (part of the National Library of New Zealand) were published in 2012 and 2016.

Merry Begins (OUP Melbourne 1947), d/w by Pat Terry. Newly-orphaned Rosemerryn Arundel (Merry) goes to her mother's old school, Tremayne's

Ladies College in Dunedin. As the story develops she helps to raise Sennen house to be the 'crack House' by the end of the term.

Merry Again (OUP Melbourne 1947), d/w by Pat Terry. Second term of Form 3. New girl Holly Stafford is a problem and brings Sennen House down, but due to the influence of Merry and her friends is a reformed pupil by the end of the book.

Merry Marches On (OUP Melbourne 1947), d/w by Pat Terry. Term three and the end of the year. Four new girls cause changes and problems, but the traditions of generations of Tremayne's pupils triumphs.

The Pen and Pencil Girls (OUP Melbourne 1948?) d/w by Pat Terry. Five girls in final year of Primary School set up a story club to write stories and poems. A competition for a group production which shows originality and co-operation inspires them to produce a book, which leads to the establishment of a Children's Page in the daily newspaper.

Juliet Overseas (OUP Melbourne and UK 1949), Australian d/w by Pat Terry, UK d/w and internal illustrations by Margaret Horder. Fifteen-year-old Juliet Harding from New Zealand attends Queen Elinor's school in England, but initially keeps secret her family's connection with the school. Due to her antipodean determination and tact, Shand House rises from slack House to 'crack House'.

Tony Against the Prefects (OUP Melbourne 1949), d/w by Pat Terry. Antonia (Tony) Frensham, in her second term at Chillingham School is full of ideas to 'rag' the prefects. Hockey, songs, classic poems, all feature in this story which shows astute understanding of schoolgirls.

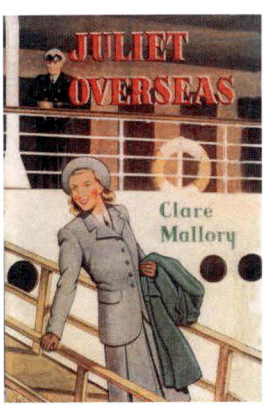

The New House at Winwood (OUP Melbourne 1949), d/w by Pat Terry. Deb Carson's first term at Winwood coincides with the establishment of a new House, Devon, despite the opposition of much of the school, and with a reluctant House Captain.

Leith and Friends (OUP UK only1950), illustrated by Kathleen Gell. Again we have a new girl settling into a large school where unruly pupils cause problems for the seniors. However, this book also has an element of unhealthy friendship but, as always, matters resolve themselves satisfactorily by the end.

The Two Linties (OUP Melbourne 1950), d/w by Pat Terry. The second book where life outside school is the main feature. Lintie Oliver lives in an orphanage, but has a second persona as Lynette Hope who displays writing talent in the Children's Page of the local newspaper.

The League of the Smallest (OUP Melbourne 1951), d/w uncredited. The new Gym Mistress began it when she lined up the school in order of height to make the croc. neat when walking to church. Housework, cooking (including making fudge), hockey, and seniors caring about juniors all feature strongly.

Candy Nevill (Margin Notes Books 2012). Nine year old Candida Nevill is dreamy and cannot live up to the high standards of her three older siblings. But she enjoys helping in the kitchen and, with the encouragement of new friends outside the family, eventually finds her talents in cooking.

Anna ~ Charlotte (Margin Notes Books 2016) Eleven year old, quiet, kind Anna is lonely when her schoolfriends take up with a flashy newcomer at school. Older Charlotte, whom Anna idolises at a distance, eventually becomes like an elder sister, taking Anna's untidiness in hand; while shy Helen sticks to Anna and they become 'best friends'

Winnie's love of food is very evident in many of her books. In **Merry Again** and also in **Candy Nevill**, the girls make sweets, including fudge and coconut ice. If you would like to imitate our heroines, here is Winnie's own 'Cocoanut Ice' recipe as printed in the Little Southlanders Page in *The Southland Times* of 21 March 1925.

COCOANUT ICE

2 cups sugar, 1 cup milk or milk and water, 1 cup cocoanut. Boil sugar and milk together till sticky – about 20 minutes. Take it off, and beat in cocoanut. When white and thick, pour half into a plate, and add a few drops cochineal to the rest, pour on top of the other, and when cold cut into squares. It is necessary to use a large pot as when the mixture is boiling it rises three or four times higher than it really is.
- Cousin Winnie McQuilkan, (11), 225 Yarrow Street, Invercargill.

An earlier version of this talk was given in 2017 to the CHOCS Conference in Wellington (CHOCS stands for Collectors and Hoarders of Old-fashioned Children's Stories.)

What Can A Girl Do in Wartime? Rosemary Sutcliff's Novels of the Romans & Beyond
Julia McLaughlin Cook

Many of you will have seen *The Eagle*, the film of 2011 based on ***The Eagle of the Ninth***. My first thought after I had seen it was, what has happened to Cottia, the girl who lived next door to Marcus? There wasn't a single speaking role for a female in the film, yet I remembered Cottia playing a big part in the novel. Straightaway I went back and reread it. My recollection was right: Cottia is quite an important character; she is a tomboy who befriends Marcus, helps him through his convalescence and looks after his dog while he and Esca travel north to find out what happened to the lost Ninth Legion. But she was not as important as I had thought: she doesn't take part in the quest at the heart of the novel, she is seen wholly through Marcus's eyes, and her main function appears to be to provide Marcus with a happy ending after his travels.

Rosemary Sutcliff was born in 1920. She was a very prolific writer of historical novels from the 1950s to her death in 1992. Her novels are at the literary end of the spectrum. They deal with serious topics, such as failure, self-sacrifice and death. They won many awards, including the Carnegie Medal for *The Lantern Bearers*. There was a shelf full of them in my local library when I was growing up, just before the books by Geoffrey Trease and Henry Treece.

I shall be looking at novels by Rosemary Sutcliff set in Britain, covering the Roman period, the Saxons, Vikings and the early Normans. I shall also consider a novel about inter-tribal fighting in Britain before the Romans arrived, and one covering a journey from Britain through the Viking world to Byzantium in the early mediaeval period/ Dark Ages. What do I mean by wartime? Invasion, full-scale battles, attacks, raids, and military occupation.

And what can a girl do in wartime? In the novels of Rosemary Sutcliff there are four main fields of activity: a girl can fight, she can endure, she can submit, and, frequently arising out of the other responses, she can be a peace-maker. Several characters take on more than one of these roles.

Cottia's role in *The Eagle of the Ninth* is typical of many of Rosemary Sutcliff's heroines. She is important to the story but she is seen only through the eyes of a male character; in fact, the only girl character in these novels who is seen from her own point of view is Frytha, in *The Shield Ring*. Often, the Rosemary Sutcliff heroine doesn't take part in the main adventure, just as Cottia, doesn't; Regina in *Dawn Wind*, for example, plays a big part in the early part of the novel but she is left behind in Britain while Owain goes across the sea for the Saxon part of the story which forms the main plot-line. And whether the girl accompanies the male character on his adventures or stays at home, she nearly always marries him at the end, which was something I had forgotten before I started re-reading.

So, let's look at what girls do in wartime. The most obvious example of a girl who fights is Boudicca in *Song for a Dark Queen*. Her life story is told by, and from the point of view of, her harper Cadvan. She is marked out for a warrior from her childhood, when she disappears from her home to follow her father and his war-host in the hope that they will let her join them. After the death of her husband and her tribe's despoiling by the Romans, it is she who sees the need to unite as many tribes as possible in order to drive out the Roman invaders before their grasp on the land becomes unbreakable. It is she who mobilises the war host, who persuades the other tribal chiefs to adopt her strategy and who leads the war host in two victories before they are overwhelmed by more disciplined Roman tactics and training. Her two daughters, Essyllt and Nessan, fight and die beside her.

Another girl who takes up arms is Frytha in *The Shield Ring*, a Saxon refugee who grows up in the last Viking stronghold of the Lake District in the early years of the Norman settlement. In addition to cooking, sewing and other womanly tasks, she learns to shoot with a bow and arrow, hunts animals for food and fights beside the men of the settlement during the course of their resistance to the Normans. What's more, Rosemary Sutcliff presents Frytha's behaviour as quite acceptable in her community:

Haethcyn glanced at the new war arrows Frytha carried thrust into her belt, and there was the grim shadow of a smile in his beard. "Did I not say to you, once on a time, that sword or distaff side, the day might come when you would have your chance to stand forth with the warbands at the Ravens' gathering?" (p. 189).

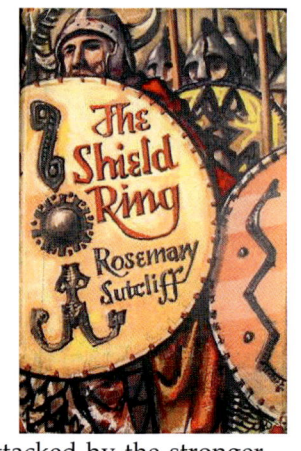

Two other royal women of the Iceni, Boudicca's tribe, take up weapons. **Sun Horse, Moon Horse**, is set in the late Iron Age, before Boudicca's time. Teleri, the sister of Lubrin Dhu, turns her hunting spear into a war spear when her tribe is attacked by the stronger Atrebates tribe:

"Make it sharp for me. Make it very sharp, Lubrin my brother." He had always thought her a soft little thing. But she showed her teeth like a young vixen.

"I will make it sharp enough to draw blood from the twilight," he said.

"So long as it will split the throat of a man!" (p. 58)

The Mark of the Horse Lord is set a hundred years after the Roman invasion, when the Iceni have relocated to south-west Scotland. Murna, the daughter of the royal woman, fights with the other young women of the tribe and the male warriors against the larger tribe of the Caledones, who are allies of Rome. Even Flavia, the well brought-up daughter of a Romanised household in **The Lantern Bearers**, snatches the dagger from her brother Aquila's belt to ward off Saxon raiders. *"Aquila saw his father fall, and with Flavia fighting like a young fury beside him, hurled himself forward against the leaping saex blades…"* (p. 39)

In **The Chieftain's Daughter**, found in the collection **Heather, Oak and Olive**, Nest does not fight with weapons but her conscience forces her to take a stand against her own people. She saves the life of the Irish captive Dara twice, first by pleading for him, and then, when pleading no longer works, by secretly helping him to escape. When the clan's priest demands another sacrifice in Dara's place, because the clan's water supply has dried up, she offers her own life instead. Fortunately, a quirk of fate means the priest does not have to put her to death.

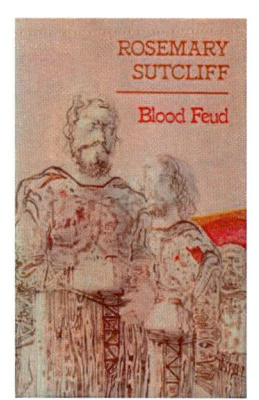

Girls who do not take up arms are called upon to endure in one way or another. This can mean keeping the home fires burning, as Frytha and Teleri and Murna do when not fighting. It's the task undertaken by most sisters and daughters and

110

friends. Alexia in **Blood Feud**, set in the Byzantine Empire in the late tenth century, helps to run the family farm part of the time. The rest of her time she spends assisting her father's medical work in the capital, patching up casualties of the Emperor Basil's wars. By acting as her father's nurse, Alexia is carrying out the traditional female role of caring for the sick. This is the role allocated to the only girl in **The Silver Branch**, who isn't even given a name:

> "Tell us what to do and we will do it," said Aunt Honoria, and it seemed to him that she was very beautiful.
>
> "Tear up your tunics," he said. "I want bandage linen; there are men here who will live if the bleeding is stopped, and d-die if it isn't. We must get the wounded together, too. Can't see what there is to do, with them scattered all up and down the hall."
>
> Other helpers were gathering to him before the words were well out; a stout wine-shop woman, a slave from the dyeworks with splashes of old dye ingrained in skin and garments; a girl like a white flower who looked as though she had never seen blood before, and many others. (p.214f.).

Another girl who tends to the sick and wounded is Princess Niamh, in **The Shining Company**. The daughter of a North British king in a post-Roman Britain facing Saxon inroads, she is learning the arts of healing from her mother. She has always loved Cynan, one of her father's warriors, and she nurses him back to health when he is the only survivor of the Saxon slaughter at Cattraeth. Sadly, her feelings are not reciprocated; Cynan, believing that her father the king abandoned him and his fellow warriors, rejects his court and sets off for Byzantium.

Regina in **Dawn Wind**, set in a 6th century Britain where the Britons are falling back before Saxon invaders, lives an unheroic life on her own terms. She grew up as a petty thief in a British city and, once it is largely abandoned after a crashing defeat, she carries on living there by herself. When she meets Owain, a survivor of the defeat, she teaches him how to survive. She only leaves with him when the arrival of raiders makes their life in the city impossible. After she is taken ill and Owain leaves her in the care of Saxon farmers she adapts to life as their servant for ten years. When the son of the household wants to take her as his second wife she asserts herself and return alone to the city of her birth, where she waits in hope for Owain's return.

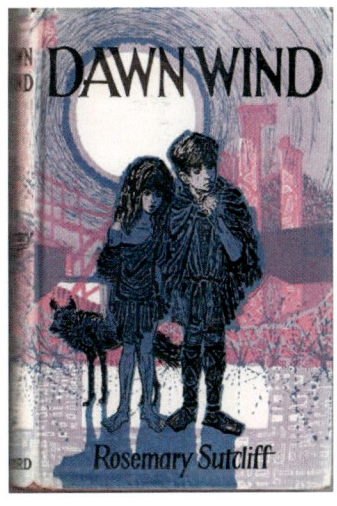

Sometimes enduring becomes more than simply going on; it means submission to a fate forced upon a girl, whether it is captivity or a husband not of one's choosing. Flavia in **The Lantern Bearers** is carried away by a Saxon raider who takes her as his wife. Years later, when she meets her captive brother Aquila by chance, she takes the risk of freeing him from Saxon enslavement but refuses to escape with him because of the son she has borne to her Saxon husband.

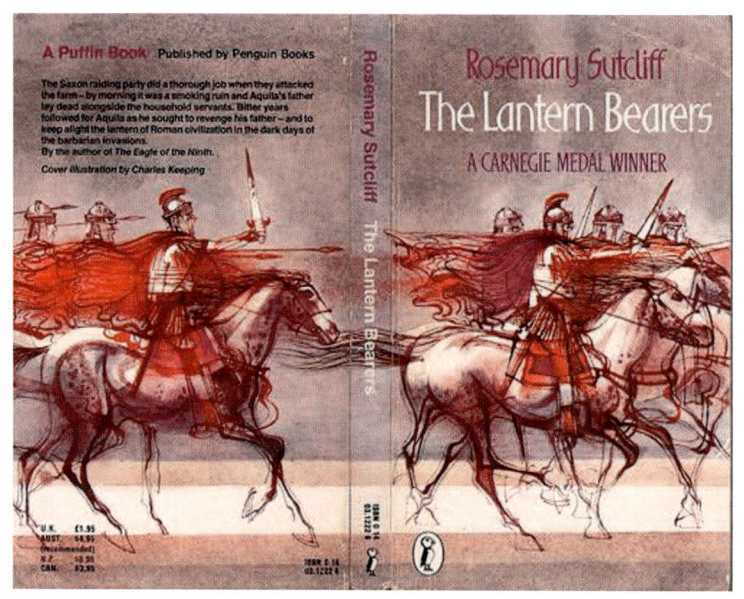

The choice of a husband and child above family and clan is made by the other girl character in **The Lantern Bearers** also. Ness, the daughter of a Welsh chief, acquiesces to marriage to Aquila in order to bind her father's tribe more closely to the British war host of Ambrosius. Like Flavia, she is seen only through Aquila's eyes. He never understands her, even after she bears him a son and he has come to care for her. Rosemary Sutcliff, however, allows the readers to see what Aquila does not, how Ness feels, and why:

>Aquila felt that he had been stupid pointing that out to her as though it were a thing she might not have noticed, when it must be so much nearer to her than to him. He wondered whether she had regretted the choice that she had made, almost thirteen years ago, but could not find the words to ask her.
>
>And then Ness came and put her thin brown hands on his shoulders and said, as though she knew what he was thinking, "Have you regretted it?"
>
>"Why should I regret it?" Aquila asked, and put his hand over hers.
>
>"I'm not beautiful like Rhianidd-"
>
>"You never were, but it was you I chose, in my rather odd way."
>
>"And maybe I've grown dull. Contented women do grow dull; I've seen it happen." She began to laugh again, and this time with no mockery at all. (p.264f.)

In ***The Mark of the Horse Lord***, Murna, the daughter of Liadhan, the Royal Lady of the Iceni, has more to endure than most: torn between her loyalty to the tribe and to her mother, who has usurped rule from the rightful chief, she witnesses the overthrow and attempted slaying of her mother; is forced into marriage to Phaedrus, the man who overthrew Liadhan; and comes to suspects that her husband is not the rightful heir to the leadership of the tribe that he claims to be. Slowly, she gets to know the man, comes to believe that he has the best interests of the tribe at heart, and refrains from betraying his secret.

These three relationships exemplify how girls can bring together two opposed communities by their marriages, even if undertaken against their wills. Girls who are not forced into such a marriage, may still not be not consulted about their choice of husband or asked for their consent: Boudicca's husband, for instance, is chosen for her out of the neighbouring tribe of the Parisi, while Frytha ponders on Bjorn's ancestress, who is said to have come "half-unwillingly" out of Wales to Cumbria.

On the other hand, some girls do have a choice: Cottia the Romanised Celt happily marries Marcus the Italian-born Briton by adoption; Frytha the Saxon takes for granted that she will marry Bjorn of Viking descent; Luned, the poor relation of a Welsh chief in ***The Shining Company***, will take Conn, the former Irish captive, with or without her kinsman's permission. And if you read ***Sword Song***, you will see that Bjorn's ancestress was also half-willing to follow his ancestor to the lake country.

This passage from ***The Capricorn Bracelet***, set in 2nd century Scotland, shows a girl making her own choice. Another Murna, the foster sister of Struan of the Votadini, welcomes the former Roman soldier Lucian Calpurnius into her home:

> And then Murna came through the inner doorway. She must have heard what passed in the smithy, and known who was there, but maybe she needed those few breaths of time…Also, she had waited to fill a cup with milk. And I mind that I noticed, even in that moment, that it was not the green glass cup, but a black pottery bowl such as she would have brought me. And I knew that Lucian was no longer a guest in the house.
>
> "Also, you promised me that if ever you were wounded, you would come to me to be made well again," she said. (p.108)

One of Rosemary Sutcliff's great themes is how the British people came into being over the centuries through the intermingling of various peoples living successively in Britain- Celts, Romans, Britons, Picts, Scots, Saxons and Vikings. This is achieved by individuals living side by side, fighting side by side, and, above all, marrying into each other's communities. This is what I mean by the fourth thing that girls can do in wartime. By marrying out into strange communities girls act as peace-makers, bringing together warring sides and laying the foundations for new, joined communities.

If you look at it that way, it isn't so disappointing that some of Rosemary Sutcliff's girl characters do not rise above being the love interest. Of course, some of you might not have thought this was a flaw; after all, for every George who wants to be a boy, there is an Anne who enjoys cooking and tidying the tent; and for every Jo can't stand lovering there is a Meg who wants a home and family of her own.

Whether you are chiefly interested in girls who fight or girls who marry, girls who care for the sick or girls who have to come to terms with a hard fate not of their choosing, you should find girls' stories to satisfy you among Rosemary Sutcliff's novels of the Making of Britain.

Bibliography
The Eagle of the Ninth, 1954
The Shield Ring, 1956
The Silver Branch, 1957
The Lantern Bearers, 1959
Dawn Wind, 1961
The Mark of the Horse Lord, 1965
Heather, Oak & Olive, 1965
The Capricorn Bracelet, 1973
Sun Horse, Moon Horse, 1977
Song for a Dark Queen, 1978
Blood Feud, 1976
The Shining Company, 1990

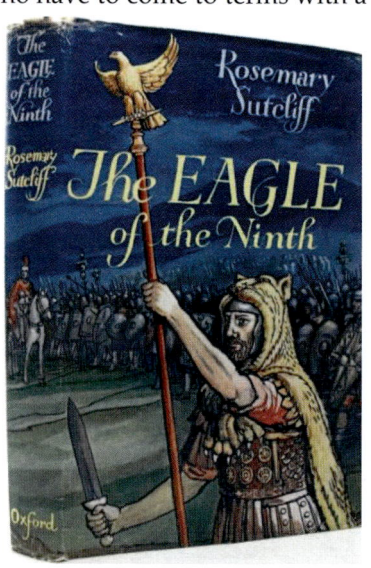

Wartime Aviatrixes: W.E. Johns and Dorothy Carter, Worrals and Marise
Stephen Bigger

My interest over the past two decades has been in stories written for children between 1939 and 1945, a time when no one knew how the war was going to turn out. I focus this paper on female flyers in fiction. The 1930s had charismatic examples of female pilots such as Amy Johnson who gripped the popular imagination. Mary Cadogan wrote a book about them in 1992, ***Women with Wings: Female Flyers in Fact and Fiction***, mostly dealing with history but linking with fictional stories. I am going to deal with two examples she mentions there, the **Worrals** books by W. E. Johns, which I shall cover in broad outline only since Mary gave a reasonable summary, and I offer a fuller discussion of the war stories of 'Dorothy Carter' (Mrs D E Heming née Eileen Marsh).

W.E. Johns and Worrals

W.E. Johns had his own experiences of flying in wartime in the Royal Flying Corps and those primitive aircraft are never far from his Biggles stories. He kept up to date through his *Flying* and *Popular Flying* magazines, and he supported Churchill in the call for rebuilding the RAF in the 1930s. Johns had been asked to interest girls in flying and encourage them into flying careers, and he knew Amy Johnson (married name Mollison, a name "Worralson" alludes to) and former stunt pilot Pauline Gower, who established the women's branch of the Air Transport Auxiliary (ATA). Paper for books was restricted, but Johns secured more than his fair share. With women being recruited into the forces, the government were keen to motivate girls and women to take an interest. There were five wartime *Worrals* books, as well as five further titles published after the war.

The wartime *Worrals* books took her far afield. The factual basis was loose. Flight Officer Joan Worralson (Worrals) of the WAAF has a friend Betty "Frecks" Lovell. WAAFs did not fly planes but Worrals flies a 'Reliant' clearly a Boulton & Paul Defiant. Frecks uses the gun turret in anger, another forbidden action for a WAAF. Two SOE-style missions to France are a stretch of the imagination too close to the truth for comfort (SOE was a secret organisation). Maybe that is why Johns was encouraged to send Worrals and Frecks further afield, to the Middle East and Australasia. He was not paid well for his books so he wrote a lot. A chapter before breakfast, he claimed, a new book in three weeks. Worrals was rather like Biggles with a bra, with similar derring-do, but she went weak at the knees when with her beau. His representation of women would not have impressed Pauline Gower.

(Dorothy) Eileen Marsh / Dorothy Carter (Mrs Heming), 1901 – 1948

My first introduction to Mrs Heming's books was through a recommendation to read Dorothy Carter's **Wren Helen** (1943), named after Eileen's daughter, with three sequels. I was fortunate to correspond with members of her family. The 1930s depression was hard on the Heming family, with four young children to feed and clothe. Eileen had a typewriter and could type well. Writing books was a possible way out. School stories were popular, boys playing cricket, girls playing hockey. Jack Heming heard in the mid-1930s that stories of flying would sell, so the couple went up to London to talk to W E Johns, then well into Biggles and his magazines about flying. They came back enthused and began to plan books on flying. Not all were happy politically. In **Blue Wings**, Jack places his heroes on the side of the Nationalists (Fascists) against the Republicans (democrats) who are stereotyped as vicious Soviets. It is a lively story, but doesn't read well today. Mrs Heming opted to use different pen-names for different audiences (and publishers). Her family helped me unravel them, as they also helped Eric Bates produce a privately printed (now unavailable) biography/bibliography **Among Her Own People: Lives and Literature of Eileen Marsh, Jack Heming and Bracebridge Heming**. Until my 2009 blog entry (in 1930-1960.blogspot.co.uk), booksellers were unaware of the pen-names.

In **Wings in Revolt** (1939), as Dorothy Carter, she includes a Captain Bigglesworthy, a humorous allusion that seems not to have annoyed her mentor. We are focusing however on Eileen's war stories including women fliers. Mary Cadogan, in *Women with Wings*, wrote: "Efforts to find out more about Dorothy Carter, as a pilot and a writer, have proved abortive – but she was certainly one of the first authors to create really convincing flying stories for girls." (p.131). By 2010 both judgements were incorrect and Mary and I met several times to discuss issues dealt with in this paper. Mrs Heming had no substantial flying experience, and was vague on details. The books also puzzled Owen Dudley Edwards in his study of Second World War youth literature. I met and corresponded with Owen around 2010 and introduced him to Bates' book and the contents of this paper.

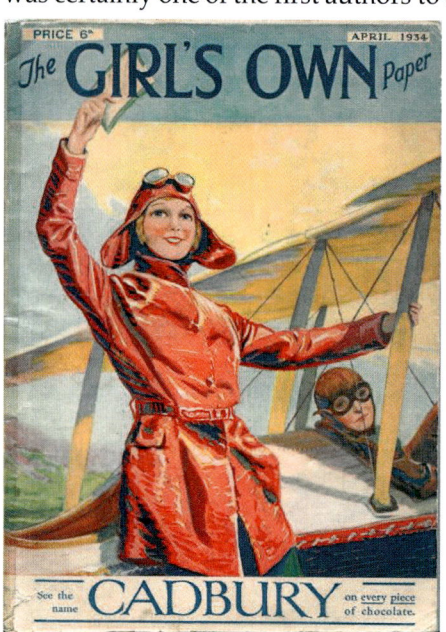

Eileen Marsh contributed frequently to the *Girls' Own Paper* (GOP) encouraging upper-middle class girls to learn to fly. From 1935 she wrote 120 books, 25 of which were about female flyers, until her death in 1948 (average 10 a year, one every five weeks) under as many as 16 names. She often combined her real names Dorothy Eileen Heming (nee Marsh) or used other family names. Altogether by 1948 there were 26 by Eileen Marsh, 14 by Dorothy Carter, 9 by Elizabeth Rogers, 8 by Guy Dempster (bloodthirsty boys' war stuff), 6 by Martin Kent, 6 by D.E. Marsh, and smaller numbers as E.M. Shard, John Annerley, James Cahill, D.E. Heming, and Dempster Heming. After the war, when paper was more plentiful, she also wrote Sunday School prizes for Lutterworth, (a lucrative market) using the names Eileen Heming, Dorothy Marsh, James Cahill, Rupert Jardine, Jane Rogers and Mary St. Helier. Her 15 adult novels, most as Eileen Marsh, offered a social commentary on the 1940s. Male names were used for boy readers, and different publishers focused on particular names. Guy Dempster books were blood-curdling Fleet Air Arm stories for boys, following troops in the armed service. The detail on Fleet Air Arm activities abroad is so precise that I suspect her husband Jack had an input while he was away on war service - the Ministry of Information book on the Fleet Air Arm, was not till 1943.

Eric Bates (p.28) sees 1939-40 as a transition from action adventure stories to well-rounded and crafted stories and novels. Certainly her adult novels begin in this period. He points to "Elizabeth Rogers"' stories (mostly with F. Warne) as a mature balance between action adventure and emotional romance. I am not dealing in detail with these books, barring a few comments on some of the novels published under a variety of names. **Rosemary, Air Pilot** is set in China featuring Japanese bombing. **The Flying Star** is a rehash of the Marise story **Star of the Air**. **The Girls of Fort Tregantle** (1946) is a romantic romp on an ATS training exercise, with the preoccupied girls giving too much away to a pair of German-Irish spies. The hot hormones wouldn't pass any feminist test today. The combination of action and romance was likely to be a commercial decision. Her adult fiction is war related and of good quality. **We Lived in London** (1942) was a hard-hitting account of life in the blitz. **The Walled Garden** (1943) began a family saga. **Eight Over Essen** (1944) followed the lives of eight members of a bomber crew who failed to return from Essen. **I Had a Son, Barbed Wire** and **The Memorial** showed village tensions.

Both Mary and Owen praise the Dorothy Carter flying stories as giving an authentic picture of flying and presume Eileen was a flier. She was not. Her first two flying books, written in 1935, were **Two Girls on the Air Trail** and **Peggy, Parachutist** in which details of how to fly were pretty imaginative, such as managing to throw a small packet from the plane into an open window. Radio tuning is usually described as 'twiddling the knobs'. When the books began to sell and she had some spare cash, she took a few short lessons to get a sense of dials and switches. She read first-hand accounts of flying and probably talked to pilots.

The series we are mainly dealing with during the war are the **Marise Duncan** titles for Collins, written as "Dorothy Carter". (There were post-war flying stories focusing on a new heroine, Jan.) The first three, although published in 1939-41, are not set in wartime, and show Marise winning the King's Cup Air Race, a kind of Schneider Trophy, then becoming a star in Hollywood, and then fighting snow and ice in the Canadian Arctic. The next three titles concern us here, **Sword of the Air** (1941), **Comrades of the Air** (1942) and **Marise Flies South** (1944). Marise has a plane at Croydon Airport and as **Sword of the Air** opens, the Second World War will be announced next day, and her secret service father is getting people out of Poland. Marise meets up with her father in between trips. Marise applies to join the WAAF (or WAFF, p.20) and is rejected but later invited to join the ATA as a ferry pilot, taking new planes from the factory to airfields. She is interviewed by a tall lady resembling Pauline Gower who developed the female section of ATA. Gowers' autobiography ***Women with Wings*** inspired Mary Cadogan's title. Amy Johnson was one of her early recruits and died on an ATA mission. The casualty rate was one in ten, but these were the glamour girls.

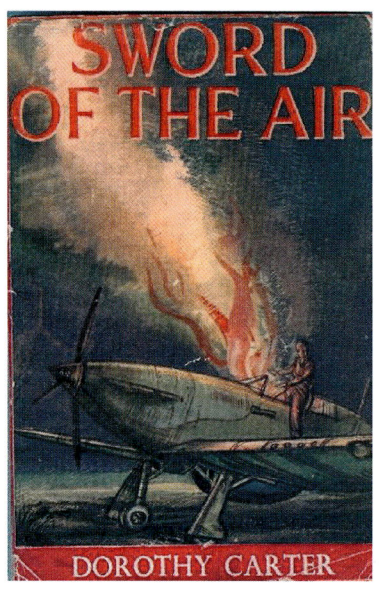

Marise's first posting is to a Hawker 'shadow factory', presumably that built on Parlaunt Farm, at Langley near Slough, developed in the late 1930s. She overcomes chauvinist banter with aplomb. Her first delivery is of a Hurricane to a camouflaged airfield (invisible from above). There was indeed a camouflage unit to deceive hostile aircrew, but such work was uncommon in 1940 when the story was set. Delivery of a four-engined seaplane to the east coast for Coastal Command gives the opportunity to describe convoy operations operating with radio silence. She begins to meet her male chums from previous adventures 'doing their bit'. She delivers a Spitfire to pre-Dunkirk France (therefore before late May 1940) where she meets two more male chums. The airfield was probably Calais Marck. The Spitfires delivered here were reconnaissance, and the story confirms that this is what her chums were doing. On the next trip her Hurricane is lost in fog and strays over German territory, brought down by flak. She hatches a mad plan to steal a Messerschmitt 109 but is apprehended. On hearing the news chum Jim goes into action. Marise feels that ordinary German soldiers are kept in the dark by propaganda, whereas the SS are 'scum of the earth' and 'scum rises to the top'. Her guide on the journey to Berlin tries to discover if she is a spy. She is kidnapped, and counter-kidnapped by the resistance, so meeting her father again. With no easy way home, Marise becomes 'Magda', cousin of an SS man working secretly with the Resistance, and is sent to work in an aircraft factory. When compromised (with prime information) she and her father are spirited away home by the three chums in night landing of a Wellington bomber.

The following year came ***Comrades of the Air***, in which Marise discovers that her three male chums are going to Russia (shortly after Barbarossa, the Nazi invasion of Russia has begun). She persuades her ATA boss (Pauline Gower in real life) to let her deliver a plane to Russia. Details of the improbable journey over German occupied territory are vague. She meets up with Russian female pilots and in particular Katya Petroff. The Soviet pilots shoot down several Nazi planes before having to close down their base in the face of enemy advances. Marise flies a 'sweet to fly' Russian bomber (Mary Cadogan surmises a Tupolev SB-2). More likely it was a Petlyakov Pe-2; Eileen was a keen reader of aircraft magazines and rejoiced in new developments. Tupolevs comprised 95% of the Russian Air Force, but it was not remotely a sweet plane to fly, quite the opposite. By 1940 it was largely obsolete though a few late versions minimised some problems. It was nicknamed Pterodactyl because its high wings were ungainly. Petlyakov was Tupolev's deputy and set to work to design a new type which entered service around 1940. The Petlyakov Pe-2 was a high-altitude twin engine bomber which came into service in 1941 and were largely flown by women pilots. It was heavy on take-off, often a two-woman job, but after that it was sweet enough to fly. It was well-defended, more so over time and from the beginning was a match for Bf109s (although gunner casualties were high).

Night witches - group portrait from 1942

The story of the Soviet women pilots has been honoured in several books, a number called "Night Witches", the name by which these female pilots were known. Most recent is Lyuba Vinogradova's ***Defending the Motherland: The Soviet Women Who Fought Hitler's Aces.*** Wherever Eileen took her information from, she told this story with deep respect.

There are various escapades, the plane losing navigation devices and ending up at the arctic coast; Marise, using her Canadian arctic skills to repair the engine, witnesses a naval war-crime, and eventually returns to habitation to find Nazi forces committing atrocities which we now know was not propaganda. Her three male chums turn up with her father, and they all overcome all odds.

In the final Marise wartime story, **Marise Flies South** (1944), she ferries planes to Darwin, Australia and New Guinea. The Australian formula was similarly used after the war for Jan (Janice) and the eponymous Wren Helen. Marise takes a B24 Liberator bomber to Darwin single-handed and is invited by two other female ferry pilots to take Typhoon aircraft to New Guinea. The story was undoubtedly suggested by the exploits of the B24 *Shady Lady*, part of the 380th Bombardment Group, "The Flying Circus". Darwin was bombed more severely than Pearl Harbour in 1942. Eleven Liberators attacked a Japanese fuel refinery on Borneo. *Shady Lady* was caught in tropical storms, flew for 16 hours 35 minutes before fuel ran out. The crew managed to patch it up enough to limp home and it became a national monument. The four-engined Liberator had a crew of ten and a range of 16 hour flying. The story assumes that Marise flies this heavy plane single-handed across the world without a co-pilot and navigator. Since the territory between India and Australia was occupied by the Japanese, there could be no refuelling half-way so the journey was impossible, something we'd better gloss over. *Jan Flies Down Under*, written four years later, details the journey with several refuelling stops including on Java, then no longer occupied by the Japanese. This story shows it to be a gruelling and dangerous journey even with a co-pilot and co-operative airfields.

Marise gets two new male chums, Pete and Babe who are shot down by the Japanese, so the girls go in to rescue them. The girls are also shot down, and finding Pete and Babe, they all have a hard time before rescue. Marise's father, posing as a German liaising with the Japanese, appears in the story from time to time. These stories for girls fore-grounded emotions and innocent romance. In all these stories the level of plausibility is low, and the detail about flying extremely rudimentary. We don't get to hear what the dials and gauges are for, or the rudder or joystick, or navigation techniques.

After the war Eileen wrote *One Woman's Life* which was a fictionalised autobiography. In this the author received a fee (£50 per book) rather than a royalty contract. This was not unusual in the 1930s (even W E Johns had to renegotiate book deals in the 1950s) and lack of royalties gave her no incentive to press for additional printings. Ten books a year would have grossed her £500 before tax, not insignificant but not a fortune. She described her writing day as starting when the children went off to school and domestic tasks completed, then on the typewriter for four hours before getting tea ready. She died of a brain haemorrhage on 5 Aug 1948 and is buried in Aldington churchyard the village of her birth. Aldington appears in many of her books about flying, a kind of personal signature.

These books are can-do books for girls. No aspiration is too high, no skill cannot be mastered. Technology is not the preserve of men. The female ferry pilots astounded airfields by having flown so many types of aircraft, including enormous 4-engined planes like Lancasters. We honour the real women who did these jobs.

[Editorial note: the ATA was actually the very first British government employment in which men and women received the same salary.]

Bibliography
Worrals series by W.E. Johns
Worrals of the W.A.A.F. (1941)
Worrals Carries On (1942)
Worrals Flies Again (1942)
Worrals on the Warpath (1943)
Worrals Goes East (1944)
Worrals of the Islands (1945)
Worrals in the Wilds (1947)
Worrals Down Under (1948)
Worrals in the Wastelands (1949)
Worrals Goes Afoot (1949)
Worrals Investigates (1950)

Dorothy Eileen Heming
As Guy Dempster (Luttterworth unless stated)
The Phantom Wing (1937, A&C Black)
Secret of the Desert (1939)
Fleet Wings (1941)
Winged Venturers (1942)

Commandos Raid at Dawn (1943)
East with the Admiral (1945)
Southward Bound (1947)
The Stolen Cruiser (1948).

As Dorothy Carter
The Marise Duncan series (all Collins)
Mistress of the Air (1939)
Star of the Air (1940)
Snow Queen of the Air (1941)
Sword of the Air (1941)

Comrades of the Air (1942)
Marise Flies South (1944)

Wren Helen series (Lutterworth)
Wren Helen (1943)
Wren Helen Sails South (1944)
Wren Helen Sails North (1946)
The Cruise of the Golden Dawn (1949)
(Latimer House)

Bates, Eric: *Among Her Own People: Lives and Literature of Eileen Marsh, Jack Heming and Bracebridge Heming* (Bulman Lee Publishing, Ashford, ISBN 0-9551014-0-9).
Bigger, Stephen; entry on Dorothy Eileen Marsh Heming, 2009; http://1930-1960.blogspot.com/2009/08/dorothy-eileen-marsh-heming.html
Cadogan, Mary: *Women with Wings: Female Flyers in Fact and Fiction* (1992)
Edwards, Owen Dudley: *British Children's Fiction in the Second World War* (2007)
Gower, Pauline: *Women with Wings* (1938)
Gradova, Lyuba: *Defending the Motherland: The Soviet Women Who Fought Hitler's Aces* (2015)
Mason, Fergus: *Night Witches* (2014) & Myles, Bruce: *Night Witches* (1981)
Whittell, Giles: *Spitfire Women of World War II* (2007)

Wartime Schools: The Chalet School and Dora Joan Potter's Winterton Series
Katherine Bruce

I love boarding school stories. To teenage me, who was miserable at school for the first half of my teen years (a not-uncommon narrative), they provided the most wonderful escapism. I found fictional friends I could believe were my own, fabulous food that I could dream of eating without even knowing what it was (it took me years to associate the tongue in my mouth with the tongue in sandwiches that sounded so delicious!), and exotic locations that I could imagine, even if I couldn't visit.

Like so many readers, I began with Enid Blyton's almost ubiquitous boarding schools: *St Clare's* and *Malory Towers*. These timeless tales were read alongside the Famous Five, Secret Seven and other Blyton titles that I had inherited from my mother. So perhaps it was unsurprising that she would launch me further along the path to reading other boarding school stories. *Exile for Annis* – her favourite book – was next, but somehow the Farm School seemed less realistic to me. (As a general rule I tend not to question authorial intent, but even at twelve I was starting to recognise the rather well-used trope of the Secret Sibling who has been There. All. Along.)

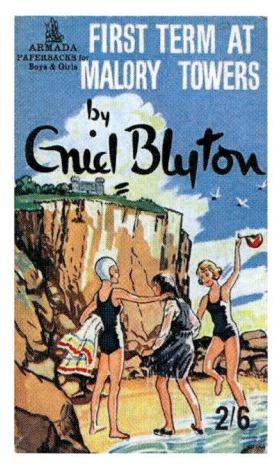

Then, in my early teens, I was introduced to Winterton School, in another boarding school series by Dora Joan Potter, which followed different groups of girls through their years at school, watching them grow and make mistakes and learn all of the usual lessons that girls in boarding school stories always do. Despite the familiar school-room setting, the girls in their brown tunics were facing a challenge that I would never truly understand – the myriad difficulties and terrors of the Second World War. The familiar combined with the completely foreign caught my attention and I became captivated with the series, which made me want to find other series that explored similar concepts. It is perhaps not a coincidence that it was also around this time that I became properly obsessed with anything and everything to do with the Second World War. I would read non-fiction books and watch documentaries endlessly on the subject.

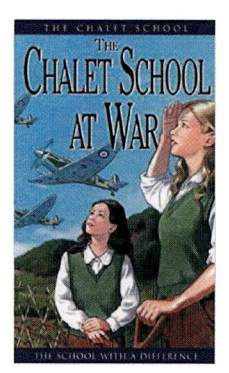

And then, at fifteen, already accustomed to the idea that even children's books could cover a subject as challenging as that one, I discovered the Chalet School series. One of the titles that first caught my attention from the list on the back of one of the Armada paperbacks was something called *The Chalet School at War*. Of course, there was no way of knowing from the title what that 'war' might be, but buoyed by the hope there was another series that dealt with the Second World War, I purchased my first of what would turn to be a very long list of books. (It is something of a relief that Dora Joan Potter stopped the Winterton series after so few titles – I doubt my bank balance would thank me for trying to track down another sixty titles!)

I dove in to the Chalet series with a heightened sense of expectation – and was delighted to find, after reading both *The Chalet School at War* and *Highland Twins at the Chalet School*, that my hopes had not been disappointed. While the two series were understandably very different, they had gentle echoes of each other in the way war-time conditions were described. There was a sense that the reader would be familiar with at least some aspects of the life that the characters were forced to lead, and yet matters were so plainly described that those who had not lived through it could easily comprehend what was happening.

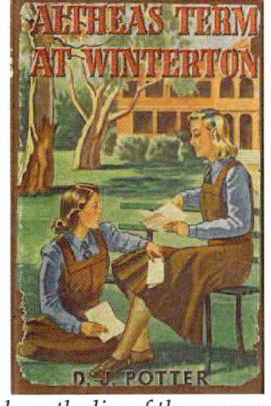

Equally importantly, factual realities of war that would have been part of the life of readers of both series were not generally over-dramatised. Rarely were the everyday hardships faced by so many used for either comic or dramatic effect. The struggles caused by rationing were shown to be affecting everyone. *"'I can't have a regular party. Rations won't allow it, you know.'"* (***Lavender Laughs in the Chalet School***) and *"'They are rationed like everything else – servants, clothes, food – '"* (***Althea's Term at Winterton***), for example. Family members and friends were mentioned as having died or been killed, and the impact of this loss was shown in a realistic manner. *"Her father hadn't come back. Those two cards which said he had been well and happy, had only been the lies of the enemy. Even before the cards had been written Dad must have been dead – dead in a prison camp!"* (***A New Girl at Winterton***) Even children were not unscathed by the horrors inflicted by the enemy.

And yet, for all that, there are differences between the two series. The first of the two reasons for this is that, while the Chalet School stories focus on the build-up to the war, the Winterton books begin in 1943, continuing until almost the end of the 1940s. This, in addition to the difference of settings in the two theatres of war, allow for interesting comparisons between the two.

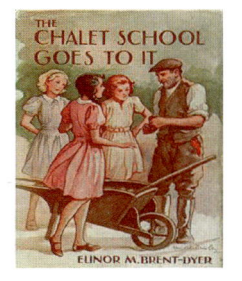

The Chalet books
The Chalet School in Exile (1940) – set in 1938/1939
The Chalet School Goes To It (1941) – set in 1940
The Highland Twins at the Chalet School (1942) – set in 1942
Lavender Laughs in the Chalet School (1943) – set in 1943
Gay From China at the Chalet School (1944) – set in 1943

The Winterton Books
With Wendy at Winterton School (1945) – set in 1943
Wendy Moves Up (1947) – set in 1945
Wendy In Charge (1947) – set in 1945/1946
Althea's Term At Winterton (1948) – set in 1946
A New Girl At Winterton (1950) – set in 1948

The ***Chalet School*** series, having existed before the war begins, is able to include hints about what is to come in books that take place several 'years' prior to the war itself. The first of these is the insightful remark in ***Exploits of the Chalet Girls*** about Thekla von Stift's brother having "*imbibed a great deal of the spirit of Young Germany*". A frivolous mention of Adolf Hitler is made several books later, in ***The New Chalet School***, when, after a rather sleepless night spent on a bus, Jo Bettany says that "*the King of England, the Pope, and Hitler*" will not get her out of bed before the following morning.

As soon as ***The Chalet School in Exile*** begins, outside events, such as the Anschluss, are immediately shown to be having a major impact on the lives of those within the school and the accompany community on the Sonnalpe. Fear and rumour-mongering is rife. It is all too clear that even the younger girls are not completely ignorant of what is happening politically across Europe. School has previously been a safe, secure environment into which external events have not really intruded in any sort of meaningful way. It becomes clear even only a few pages into *The Chalet School in Exile* that this is no longer the case.

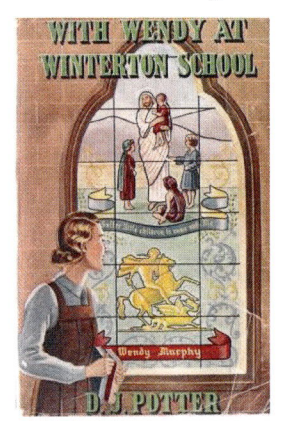

Meanwhile even the first few pages of *With Wendy at Winterton School* contain many hints and glimpses into the world of wartime Australia. There is a touching description of a *"middle-aged driver [who] jumped perceptibly in his seat. He was a returned soldier and his nerves were not in the best condition."* The Americans are described as "doing well in the Pacific". There is talk about the war on the radio. And the central character of the early books, Wendy Murphy, is suitably scornful of the fact that valuable inches of the newspaper are devoted to the return to school of Felicity Filmore-Danvers, *"In war-time too!"* As well as setting up the central conflict of the first book, this singular mention gives the reader a glimpse into the character of Wendy Murphy and her appreciation of the world outside the safety of school – and wartime constantly intrudes into this safe circle throughout the series, just as it does to the Chalet School.

However it is not just the girls whose views are taken into account. One area for which the Chalet School is frequently praised is in its depiction of scenes among the adults in the books, without girls or children being present. Such scenes allow Elinor Brent-Dyer to offer a more grown-up attitude to what is happening in the wider world, for instance in the discussion of Hitler's plans for Germany in *The Chalet School in Exile*, or the reference to Mary Burnett's people having been "bombed out", or when the former Miss Durrant, now Mrs Redmond, returns to school to teach following the death of her daughter in an air raid. Dora Joan Potter includes similar glimpses into the lives of the school's mistresses, showing the losses they suffered, and which would have been so familiar to the books' readers.

Of course there were some in the school who could never forget. The form-mistress of the Remove was one. Engaged to a successful, young architect at the outbreak of war, her marriage had been postponed by his enlistment six months later and twelve months after that he had been reported killed in the Middle East. Miss Carrington, bereft of that which she had held most dear could never forget the misery and desolation of the war. Mademoiselle, the French mistress was another. She never knew what became of her father and brothers and sisters after France fell. (**With Wendy at Winterton School**)

Both schools are also shown to be providing their support to both local and international movements playing a role in the war. The Chalet

School has always been shown to provide assistance to local worthy causes, but now that the need is shown to be greater, and on a wider basis, both schools put their work into helping the Red Cross, as well as local hospitals or other needy groups. In the Chalet School, for example, "*He cut his speech very short, merely saying that all present knew it was in aid of the Red Cross. As this was a Nativity play, there must be no applause from beginning to end.*" (**Highland Twins at the Chalet School**), while "*A series of fetes, Paddy's markets and concerts had been arranged to assist the grown of the ambulance fund... And then, last but not least, there was the gymkhana, held annually at Winterton to aid the cot supported by the school at the Children's Hospital.*" (**With Wendy at Winterton School**) And "'*the House shield... Miss Lethbridge started the idea in 1940, mainly to encourage our efforts towards raising funds for patriotic purposes.*'" (**Wendy Moves Up**)

Thus far the two series have had a number of similarities, but one area worth examination in the attitude towards Germans. Perhaps because of her own experiences in Austria, or because she had established a community of those who were soon to be England's enemies, Elinor Brent-Dyer ensures that her characters do not tar all Germans with the same brush. In **The Chalet School in Exile** is this explicit statement: "'*Gottfried! It isn't you; it's the Nazis. We don't blame you; we don't even blame the German people for all this...But never think that we blame you. We've lived in Tyrol too long for that!*'" Of particular relevance is the speech by Emmie Linders in which she explains how the rise of Nazism has caused German women to rethink the traditional desire to have children.

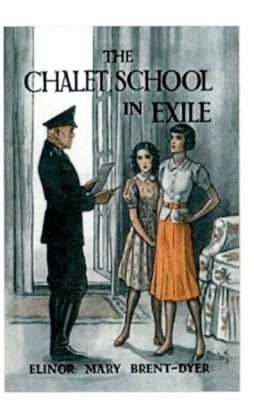

> '*They were of the old Germans, who loved the home, and music, and brought us up to do the same. But the Nazis leave one no home. They take the children from their parents when they are yet too young to know, and teach them their own wicked thoughts. Many of our old girls have wedded and now have children, and once every good German Mädchen hoped the day would come when she, too, would have babies. I hoped it might never come, for my children would be taken from me, and taught things I hate and know to be evil!*' (**Highland Twins at the Chalet School**)

Given that, prior to this point in the series, Elinor Brent-Dyer sends most of her Continental girls straight into marriage from school, this shows the dramatic shift in attitudes caused by the war.

The creation of the Peace League further emphasises the difference between Germans and Nazis, reminding even the youngest girls, and also the reader, that not all Germans embraced Nazism.

> '*We, the girls of the Chalet School, hereby vow ourselves members of the Chalet School Peace League. We swear faithfully to do all we can to promote peace between our countries. We will not believe any lies spoken about evil doings, but we will try to get others to work for peace as we do. We will not betray this league to any*

enemy, whatever may happen to us. If it is possible, we will meet at least once a year. And we will always remember that though we belong to different lands, we are members of the Chalet School League of Peace.' (**The Chalet School in Exile**)

Dora Joan Potter has somewhat different but evolving opinions. In her first book, published in 1945, her dislike of Germans is all too clear. "'*He's a German, isn't he? All Germans are cruel! The Germans killed my Daddy!*'" (**Wendy in Charge**) The Germans are blamed for the deaths of key characters and for the destruction of one character's home in England. By the time of the final book, published in 1950, perhaps reflecting the general shift towards the Germans that was beginning during that period, Dora Joan Potter also allows for a change.

"'During the war there were Germans who obeyed the rules laid down by Hitler because if they didn't they would have been killed. But that is not to say that they were Nazis... for they never, in their inmost hearts, accepted Hitler as their leader nor Hitler's way nor Hitler's friends as theirs.'" (**A New Girl at Winterton**)

In fact, she contradicts or conveniently forgets some of her characters' earlier actions when she later says the Winterton girls have treated their German master well. Potter reflects Elinor Brent-Dyer's ability to differentiate between Nazis and Germans in the final book when she has one of the characters reflect how his wife was not a Nazi.

While that gives an overview of general views towards Germans and Nazis, it is worth examining how individual characters are treated. There are two interesting examples in Elinor Brent-Dyer's books: Frau Mieders has appeared in several books prior to the war books and she is a clearly beloved character so it is perhaps unsurprising that, although she is initially unable to leave with the rest of the school, she reappears by the time of **Lavender Laughs in the Chalet School**, having escaped together with her younger sister who is said to have now joined one of the Women's Forces. Frau Mieders is not mentioned again in the war-time books, but that is perhaps more to do with the fact that rationing would have made cooking and cleaning classes difficult than because of the mistress's nationality.

The other noteworthy German character in the war-time books is Frau Eisen, the woman who spies on the group as they attempt to hide the Peace League document. It is interesting that Elinor Brent-Dyer gives Frau Eisen other personality traits than mere love of Nazism: she eavesdrops on girls on the train, is rude when she comes to visit Madge, and forces her son to go in search of the Chalet School party without her, promising to thrash him when he gets home for using the Nazi greeting. She then reports them to the authorities, and given the negative view of telling tales that has been prevalent through the rest of the series, this helps to confirm her status as an enemy.

In stark contrast to this is the treatment accorded to Herr Brendt, the German master at Winterton. It is implied that he has been at the school for a long time, and yet the suspicion of him means that most girls are no longer allowed to be tutored by him so he has little money. While this is perhaps something of a natural attitude for the time, it is interesting that, in a book published in 1947, Herr Brendt is treated very cruelly by many of the girls, even the most senior of them. The hiding of his glasses, which leaves him vulnerable, is described by some of those girls participating in the prank as reasonable. It takes a new girl to the school, when remarking on the ringleader of the prank, to say that, "*Ten years at Winterton and all she can show for it is a tendency to distress and humiliate a broken old man – yes – a broken old man, without even a country to call his own!*"

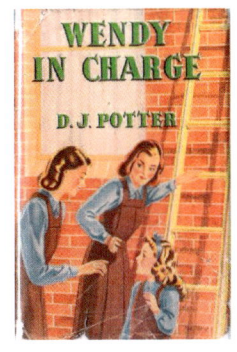

Of course, Australia had an enemy much closer to home than the Germans, and it is not surprising that the Japanese would feature largely in the first book of the series, the only one published during war-time. Here Dora Joan Potter makes use of a trope that was prevalent on both sides of the world: the idea that the enemy would make use of nuns' habits to disguise their movements. The scene that follows Wendy's discovery of this concealment is almost ludicrous in its exaggerations, and, from a twenty-first century perspective, uncomfortable in its blatant racism.

Wendy looked curiously at the black-robed figures opposite. … Those bulky dresses and starched wimples! How hot they must be! And what big thick boots they wore – good gracious!

Wendy sat forward slightly, her eyes caught by those boots. Surely they were brown boots – surely – why – Wendy's eyes dilated – surely they were men's military boots! Now why in the world would nuns wear military boots?

And then those discordant voices jarred on her ears again and she sat back fearfully in her seat again, her heart, as those voices became lower, thumping and heaving in her chest. A sudden wild knowledge came to her – instinctive knowledge, for Wendy had never heard that language before – the knowledge that the 'nuns' opposite were speaking – Japanese! And Australia was at war with Japan! Military boots – Japanese language – what could it mean but that, sitting opposite Wendy Murphy in a hills train, were none other than two Jap spies disguised as nuns!

Even as the realization came to her, Wendy felt revolted. To use the holy habit of a nun as a disguise! She felt disgusted, sick and frightened at the one moment and wondered wildly what she should do…

'Spies! Japs!' she hissed undiplomatically. She grasped frantically at their flowing robes. Then – as a sharp pull tore the hoods from two shaven heads she saw their faces – yellow faces, shrewd and brutal with the slanting eyes of their race – and at the moment, contorted with a mixture of fear and fury. The tall one gave an exclamation in a strange language and the short one caught Wendy's arm suddenly and thrust his enraged face into hers.

'Australian pig-child!' His fingers were like a vice on her arm. *'Australian pig-child mind her own business!'*

For an author writing to appeal to a market saturated by such anti-Japanese sentiment, however, attitudes and descriptions such as those included in the book would have been quite reasonable. Hatred of the enemy, particularly in 1943 with the war still very much hanging in the balance, was a not unreasonable excuse for the inclusion of such descriptions.

One subject that is touched on by both authors, but which may have caused either confusion or controversy among their readers, is the question of concentration camps. Both authors include references to these horrors, which help to drive forward the plot of two books - **The Chalet School in Exile** and *A New Girl at Winterton*. It is Elinor Brent-Dyer who deserves greater accolades here for their inclusion, as so little was known definitively in 1938-9 when her book was written and set. Readers of the Chalet School, and Elinor Brent-Dyer herself, could only guess what was behind such seemingly innocuous terms as special treatment or resettlement. Among several references are "'*I love my country, but I will not stay to see her disgraced by secret imprisonments, maltreating of Jews — though I have no real love of Jews, they have the right to live and prosper with any of us — and concentration camps,*'" and "*Both young men had been in one concentration camp, though both refused to say much about it. They had endured tortures, and had known cold and semi-starvation for months. Knocked about and brutally beaten for the slightest offence, the wonder was that they had survived.*"

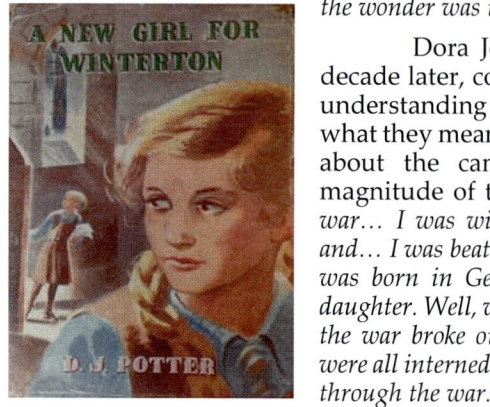

Dora Joan Potter, writing more than a decade later, could do so with the benefit of full understanding of what the camps involved and what they meant. Thus when her readers are told about the camps, they understand the full magnitude of their horrors. "'*I was a prisoner of war... I was with the Germans... I was ill-treated and... I was beaten unconscious,*'" and "'*Grand-dad was born in Germany and so was Mummy – his daughter. Well, we were holidaying in Germany when the war broke out. Because Daddy was English we were all interned at Grunsenn, and there we stayed all through the war.*'"

It is perhaps interesting that the question of Jews in death camps does not appear in either book. The abuse and murder of Herr Goldmann in **The Chalet School in Exile** is certainly the closest either author comes to mentioning the Holocaust directly. Dora Joan Potter fails to mention the subject at all. This was, of course, typical for the time; the Holocaust was generally not spoken of during the late 1940s and 1950s, and would certainly not have featured in a children's boarding school series.

There is one final point in which the two series diverge: the question of the beginning and end of the war. Elinor Brent-Dyer does not address the issue of the declaration of war, although she states numerous times that war is coming. Finally, she is unable to hold it back any longer, "*Reminding them that Britain was at war*". Her books show the progression of the war - but the title published in 1945, ***Jo to the Rescue***, contains little that is war-related. Rationing seems not to exist. Travel is not an issue. There is no black-out. The title that follows this, ***Three Go to the Chalet School***, which did not appear until 1949, does contain a character who is staunchly anti-German, but it is never clearly stated why this is so. Later books in the series do make reference to the horrors of war, but Elinor Brent-Dyer never touches on the mixed feelings that would have greeted the defeat of both German and Japanese enemies.

Naturally Dora Joan Potter cannot include the topic of the war's beginning in a series that only begins in 1943, but it has always been a matter of great personal satisfaction to me that she instead chose to pay a significant amount of attention of the end of the war. The second book in the series, ***Wendy Moves Up***, devotes an entire chapter to the celebration of this great event, showing it to be both a joyous and an emotional occasion.

> *Mary clicked the dial and waited for the set to warm up. She turned to address a remark to Wendy, but it was stifled before it ever reached her lips, for, at that moment, the news – the glorious, wonderful, tremendous news they had all been waiting for – had given up hope of hearing – that news came through at half past eight on the 15th August, 1945!*
>
> *All over their vast continent of Australia; all over their Motherland itself; all over the great country of their American cousins; all over the war-wracked country of their ally China; yes all over the whole wide world, the official news of the surrender of Japan was broadcast at that moment! And everywhere hearts moved in an instant prayer of thankfulness and gratitude, just as many hearts at Winterton School also moved. There was one stupendous moment of silence and then cheer upon cheer rent the 'Waratah' dining-room!*
>
> *"The war is over! The war is over! The war is over! Hip! Hip! HURRAH!"*
>
> *Wendy clasped Mary and waltzed her round the tables; Rosemary grabbed Gillian and did an unprecedented thing – she kissed her! Beryl, Gerry and Rae jumped up and down and sent a porridge plate flying – porridge and all! But no one minded! Delia grabbed the person nearest to her and did a whizzy round and round, before she realised that it was no other than the patrician Miss Chumley!*
>
> *But Miss Chumley, with tears rolling down her face unchecked, no longer seemed to remember that she was either a House Mistresss or an alleged aristocrat. She was one of a great people – a people who had helped to make this moment possible – a great people whose women and children and old men had fought on the home*

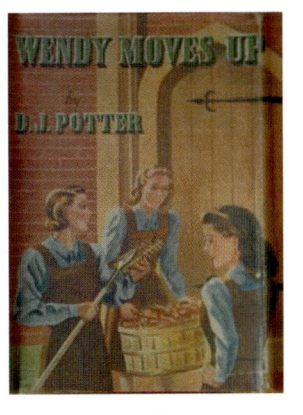

front, fighting the fires and standing the strain of nights and days of bombing...

Of particular note is the list of nations who are acknowledged as being permitted to join in the celebrations: the acknowledged allies of America and Britain, along with Australia. But they also cheer Russia and China, nations with whom they would soon be in conflict. Dora Joan Potter chooses not to make reference to these later conflicts, although Elinor Brent-Dyer hints at it when referring to Russia's occupation of Austria in ***Carola Storms the Chalet School*** and its *'present frame of mind'* in ***Changes for the Chalet School***.

As a snapshot of history, both the Chalet School and the Winterton series are valuable for readers. For contemporary readers, it allowed them to appreciate that even fictional characters were sharing the same challenges and sufferings that the readers themselves were experiencing. Modern-day readers can make use of the books as a valuable historical document, as long as they remember that the authors were writing at or to close the time when their books were set, and thus they cannot reasonably be considered in the light of twenty-first century attitudes. Instead they can be valued for what they are: a telling of special stories in a unique period of history which has so much to teach us even more than seventy years after it.

Entertaining Evacuees
Sue Sims

There are scores, probably hundreds of books in which evacuees play a part, and there's a definite limit on what one can cover in a short talk. Here, then, are the parameters I used when researching the topic:
- the book had to be published during or immediately after WW2, and given the normal turn-around time before a book hits the shops, this meant a publication date between 1940 and 1947
- only girls' school stories or Guide stories qualified
- the book had to focus on or mention evacuees.

These criteria excluded a large number of books – for example: Violet Methley's ***Vackies*** – plenty of evacuees but not a school or Guide story; Heather White's ***Rowan in Search of a Name*** – Guides, but no evacuees; ***Lavender Laughs at the Chalet School*** – girls' school story but also no evacuees; and ***School for Skylarks*** by Sam Angus: a girls' school with evacuees, but published in 2017.

I've also separated Guide stories from school stories – or rather, they proved to be completely distinct between these dates. While early Guide books are generally school stories as well (the very first Guide story, ***Terry, the Girl Guide*** [1912], was not only set in school but also part of a school story series by Dorothea Moore) by 1939, they were separate genres with only occasional cross-overs.

This paper, then, will start with school stories before moving on to Guides. They divide into two types: Schools which are evacuated and schools which stay in their original location but deal with evacuees or refugees.

Category 1: There are quite a few books which feature evacuated schools – I've found ten of them, and there may well be more. They range from books which no one's ever heard of, like Olive Duhy's 1946 *Esme and the Smugglers* and *The Mallowfield Trail* by Norman Pugh (1944), to the two Chalet books (*The Chalet School in Exile* and *The Chalet School Goes to It* – though the former has a refugee school rather than an evacuated one) and several Angela Brazils. In most cases, the evacuations are rather pointless from a plot point of view: the schools frequently end up in Tudor mansions or ancient castles with useful secret passages or priests' holes, but the books could easily have been established in those buildings from the outset: many pre-war books did just that, and one suspects that the various authors used the evacuations simply to sound relevant and up-to-date. But there are a few books where the evacuation is basic to the plot.

First, there are the books where two schools are evacuated to the same building (something that seems to have happened quite frequently in the first year of the war). There are plenty of books, of course, which use a 'combined school' plot, both before and after the war, such as EBD's *The New Chalet School* (not to mention later books such as *Bride Leads the Chalet School* or *Feud in the Chalet School*). Evacuation meant that writers didn't have to invent reasons for school A to join school B: it was a realistic and recognisable event. The war isn't particularly important, for instance, in Brazil's *The Secret of the Border Castle*: after the first few pages, which establish the situation, it's like any other 'combined school' story, focusing on the gradual reduction of hostility between the two sets of pupils, plus the common school story theme of the search for a missing will. Two books which stand out here are Norah Mylrea's *Spies at Candover*, her 1941 sequel to the pre-war *Unwillingly to School*: Candover plays host to an evacuated school, St Ann's, and there's a fair amount of hostility between the two groups of girls. (It's unclear why St Ann's has to be evacuated and Candover doesn't, since although St Ann's is *'on the Hampshire coast'*, they and Candover are *'only a few miles apart'* [p.13].) Admittedly, the clashes between pupils soon take a back seat to the spy plot indicated by the title (spoiler alert: the evil German agent is Miss Carter, the new Maths teacher) – very few children's authors managed to resist the temptation of introducing spies into their war books.

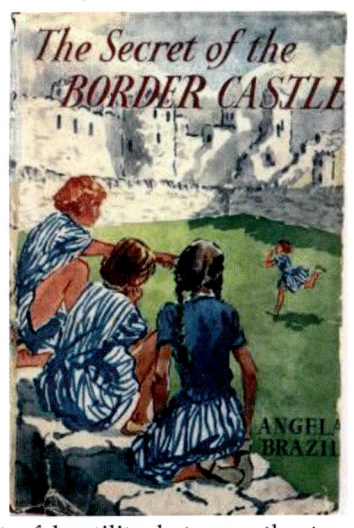

The other interesting book is very different. In W.W. Eastways' *Girls of Greycourt* (the 1944 sequel to *Greycourt* [1939]), the story is episodic, focusing mainly on the protagonist Jill, who moves during the book from the Fourth Form into the Sixth. The war begins about three-quarters of the way through the book, as does the evacuated school plot – funnily enough, it's another St Anne's, though with an E this time, à la Anne Shirley. There's no hostility between the schools in this case, though this may be because the St Anne's girls are billeted with local families: the only conflict (it's a very gentle book) is between one of the St Anne's girls and the woman with whom she's billeted: *"[Sheila] is unhappy at her billet...She's just made to feel what a trouble she is, and what large appetites schoolgirls have, and how it has lowered the tone of the place to have evacuees here."* [p191]

All the other St Anne girls are *"all so happy."* [p.191]. I think this is almost the only example I've found in contemporary school or Guide stories of an evacuee who's been badly treated in any way, though there are plenty which focus on the difficulties of their hosts. There's a passing reference in another 'combined school', found in Brazil's ***Five Jolly Schoolgirls*** (1941) (of all the books I found, perhaps the one which gives the best flavour of what it was like to be an evacuated schoolgirl), where Eva tells the other girls: *"[Our digs] are horrid. Dilys and I are going to ask Miss Glover to change us somewhere else. We can't stand it, can we, Dilys?"* [p.41] But we don't get any more information about Eva and Dilys's digs. And though this is a 'combined school', Brazil's not really interested in either clashes or friendships between the two groups: the girls evacuated from Dunford High School – among whom are the eponymous Five Jolly ones – only encounter the Greenfield College girls in lessons, and almost all the focus is on their leisure activities.

Let's move on to the second part of the 'school' taxonomy – schools which aren't themselves evacuated, but which encounter non-scholastic evacuees. And here we come to one of the major themes of this paper: the way in which evacuees are defined and viewed by contemporary writers. With very few exceptions (dealt with below), books written during this period – as, indeed, more recently – focus on the London working-class evacuees, often from the slums, and their interaction with residents of the small towns and villages with whom they were billeted. In fact, industrial cities all over the country, and large east and south coast towns and ports, all took part in the 1939 evacuation; and plenty of middle-class children were sent away from home, some with their schools (as noted above), but others as individuals staying with family or friends in the country or towns in the west of England, initially thought to be reasonably safe from air-raids. But the slum-child-in-the-country motif made for better stories – more contrast, more conflict, and also more humour, generally at the expense of the ignorant and untrained evacuees. One of the best examples is from ***The Chalet School Goes To It*** (1941), where the prefects are recounting stories they've heard about the evacuees: Brent-Dyer notes that *'most of them were city children who, coming from poor areas, knew nothing about the country, and their comments were unconsciously humorous in the extreme.'* It's probable that

Brent-Dyer is passing on stories she'd heard second- or third-hand in Hereford, as they do ring true. Here's one of them:

> "Well, Mr Rosser was taking the kids round the place, and in the orchard they came across one of those famous white sows of his – ringed, of course. You know how they bark the trees if they're not."
>
> The Prefects nodded...
>
> "Well," went on Gwladys, who was rather addicted to this opening gambit, "the smaller boy wanted to know why the piggy had a ring through its nose. Before Mr Rosser could say anything, he got his answer – from his brother. 'Don't yer know thet? Thet's becorse it's married, of course." [p.128]

The prefects decide to throw a party for the evacuees: we don't hear any more of this, which is a shame, though rather typical of EBD. It's representative, though, of the attitude of most children's authors at this period towards evacuees: contemptuous at worst, and a rather patronising pity at best. Going back to *Girls of Greycourt*, Jill encounters three evacuees billeted with an adult friend: they've littered the house and garden, are rude and demanding, and never do any household tasks. The girl, who's thirteen, only likes "the pictures, but there aren't any in this old – ". Jill scolds them, but also promises to take them to the pictures – presumably the equivalent of the Chalet prefects giving a party for the evacuees. It's the same attitude – always kindly, but unmistakably that of superior to inferior.

The fascinating thing is that, when one moves over to Guide stories, this condescending attitude largely disappears. The evacuees in these books are still clearly working-class Londoners: the authors make this quite clear through the use of eye dialect [a visual indication of the speaker's non-standard dialect or poor education made apparent by using occasional non-standard spellings, such as "wos" for was and "sed" for said - ed]. But the evacuees are Guides, and the authors of these books, who were themselves heavily involved with Guiding, take quite seriously the fourth Guide Law: "A Guide is a friend to all and a sister to every other Guide." Social class isn't glossed over, but it's presented as irrelevant to the sisterhood.

A good place to begin is with *Two Rebels and a Pilgrim*, published in 1941. The author, Margaret Tennyson, editor of The Guider, used the pseudonym 'Carol Forrest' for this and her other children's books, all of which focus in some way on Guiding as a spiritual as well as a practical way of living. Towards the end of this book, 14-year-old Chris and 13-year-old Penny, who have been on a walking tour with Penny's aunt when war breaks out, are trying to return to London when they're mistaken for evacuees. More or less captured, they're locked in overnight in an empty school building with dozens of real evacuees:

Penny sighed explosively. "It's not as if we even looked as if we were evacuees," she said plaintively. "Do we look as if we'd just come from London with all our things for a long stay! All the others have at least got suitcases an' – an' things with them. You'd think anyone could see we were different, wouldn't you?"

"Um – I s'pose it's just that they're all worried stiff and excited, and tired. Oh – shut up, Joan – for goodness' sake!" [Joan is one of the evacuees also temporarily billeted in an empty school building.]

"I want me Mum!" Joanie wailed. "I did tell Dad I'd look after 'er 'fore 'e went off to 'is ship. An' now she ain't got nobody." [pp95-6 of the book]

Two things to notice here: first, the class distinction (shown by Joan's accent) – that, as we've seen, is absolutely standard. The second, however, becomes clear in the subsequent conversation, where Joan helps Chris and Penny to escape with a home-made rope, while eventually agreeing to stay evacuated herself because:

"Your orders are to stay here," Chris said uncomfortably.

There was a silence, a long rigid silence, then "And to obey the Guide Law'," Joanie muttered under her breath. "Oh – heck, and it says you've got to 'elp others too!" [p.97]

And it's Joanie who makes a rope out of blankets in the dark (*"I'm not champion knotter for nothing. Always did like competitions in the dark. You get your fings ready and get dressed, leave the knots to me."* [p.98])

This is, then, the biggest difference between the school stories which deal with evacuees and their Guide equivalents: while class distinction is never ignored, the evacuated London Guides frequently turn out to be better Guides – more efficient, more committed, and more obedient to the Guide Law.

Catherine Christian, editor of *The Guide* and close friend of Margaret Tennyson/Carol Forrest, wrote several books dealing with Guiding during the war, two of which feature evacuees. In **The Seventh Magpie** (published in 1946, but set shortly before the end of the war), the youngest of the Magpie patrol, Emily, is an evacuee from London. Christian uses eye dialect for her speeches (*"What's wrong with her, anyway? I seen 'er in Mrs. Wiggs' shop the other day. Looks kind of ferocious at you, don't she?"* [p.12]), but she's otherwise just a normal member of the patrol, if a rather untidy one: there's no sense that she's inferior to the other members. More interestingly, **The "Kingfishers" See it Through** (1942) opens (more or less) with a meeting to discuss the disbandment of the Guide company in favour of a 'Youth Squad' in the local independent school. Christian contrasts the superior Margaret, patrol leader of the Bullfinches, who's all in favour of the exclusive Youth Squad, and Elvira, the leader of the London Pride patrol comprising evacuees. Elvira and her patrol *"haven't been satisfied, not in a long while we haven't. We've been right down disappointed, if you want to know."* They see the country Guides as "stuck up", and complain that the latter don't bother with *"camping and woodcraft and that. We want to learn things."* The narrator, Sylvie, notices *"how shabby [Elvira's] old camp overall looked beside the fresh, ironed smartness of Margaret's. And yet, in some odd way, it looked as if it belonged to her, and she in it, as Margaret never looked in uniform."* [pp.19-20]

Another interesting book in this area is **Merrily Makes Things Move** (1942), by Dorothy Osborn Hann, better known for her long series of books about Peg and her patrol, based on Mrs Hann's own troop in Walworth, south-east London. In **Merrily Makes Things Move**, the eponymous protagonist and her older sister Rosemary have to spend the summer holidays with their aunt, who's married to the rector of a church in the village of Haddington-on-the-Hill. The rectory initially hosts several evacuees, including 12-year-old Tilly and her two younger brothers: Tilly, an unabashed Cockney (her reaction to picking currants is *"Coo! They aren't half sour!"* [p.29]), is a Guide, and her efficiency and usefulness around the house are contrasted with Rosemary's reluctance to do any housework and general snobbishness (*"Not that she knew anything about Girl Guides, but if Tilly was one she was sure she would not like them."* [p.29]). Mrs Hann isn't starry-eyed about evacuees in general – later in the book, the rectory takes in a young mother and her baby who *'evidently considered herself a guest of the Government, and as such seemed to expect that most of the work would be done for her!'* [p.91] But Tilly the Guide is admirable throughout.

There is, admittedly, a rather strange book by Heather White called **Watersmeet** in which the evacuee protagonist, 13-year-old Mariska, from a broken home and a very reluctant Guide, is guided (so to speak) along the right path by upper-class Jocelyn. But it's the exception that proves the rule: overall, in school stories, evacuees are to be helped and patronised; in Guide stories, they're the ones doing the helping.

Overall, then, considering modern sensibilities, Guides definitely win!

Bibliography of Wartime School and Guide Titles
Angela Brazil: *Five Jolly Schoolgirls* (1941); *The Mystery of the Moated Grange* (1942); *The School in the Forest* (1944); *The Secret of the Border Castle* (1943)
Elinor M. Brent-Dyer: *The Chalet School in Exile* (1940); *The Chalet School Goes to It* (1941); *Highland Twins at the Chalet School* (1942); *Gay from China at the Chalet School* (1944)
Catherine Christian: *Harriet Takes the Field* (1942); *The "Kingfishers" See it Through* (1942); *The School at Emery's End* (1940); *The Seventh Magpie* (1946): reissued as *Sally Joins the Patrol* (1948)
Gwendoline Courtney: *The Denehurst Secret Service* (1940); *Well Done, Denehurst* (1941)
Olive C. Dougan: *Schoolgirls in Peril* (1944) (begins in school); *The Schoolgirl Refugees* (1940) (begins in school)
Olive Duhy: *Esme and the Smugglers* (1946)
W.W. Eastways: *The Girls of Greycourt* (1944)

Josephine Elder: *Strangers at the Farm School* (1940)
Rosemary Forde: *Cherry Jam at Glencastle* (1946)
Carol Forrest: *Patteran Patrol* (1944); *Two Rebels and a Pilgrim* (1945); *The House of Simon* (1942)
Mrs A.C. Osborn Hann: *Merrily Makes Things Move* (1942)
Mary K. Harris: *Gretel at St Bride's* (1941)
Agnes Miall: *The Schoolgirl Fugitives* (1942) (begins in school)
Norah Mylrea: *Spies at Candover* (1941)
F.O.H. Nash: *Lucy of the Sea Rangers* (1943)
Norman Pugh: *The Mallowfield Trail* (1944)
Heather White: *Watersmeet* (1940); *Rowan in Search of a Name* (1941)

Book Launch: Career Novels for Girls
Kay Clifford

Kay Clifford, as Kay Whalley, has spoken at past Bristol conferences, including talking about career novels at the 2012 conference. We were delighted that her new book, "Career Novels for Girls" was launched at this conference. Here Kay introduces her book:

Those lovely career books of the 40s and 50s with their alliterative titles: Rennie Goes Riding; Cookery Kate; Shirley: Sales Assistant; Chris at the Kennels. If you were named Ann, you could aspire to be Air Hostess Ann. Except that you had to be Grammar School educated (which immediately narrowed the field), stand over 5'2", weigh between 105lbs and 135lbs and understand that you'd be sacked as soon as you got married. And, of course, every girl expected to get married, didn't she? A career was only for those years between Leaving School and Finding A Man.

So most of us, in spite of those glorious and uplifting career books, became a Secretary or a Nurse. Or a Teacher if you were clever. Or even a Librarian if you were really clever (for a girl, that is). Some of us, reading those Bodley Head or Chatto & Windus career books yearned to be a Ship's Officer, or a farmer, or the Captain of a Ship, or drive cars while our husbands did the housework (yes, there is one book – but only one book – where this happens) but we didn't and couldn't.

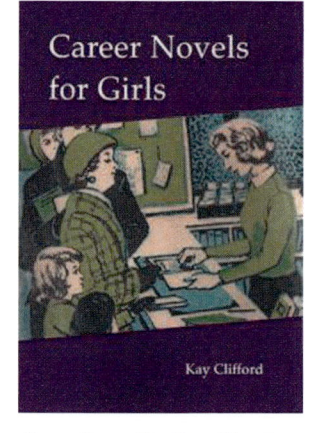

It would be 40 years before Eileen Nolan would be an Army Brigadier, and 50 years before entry into Medical Schools would be 50% female. But these books opened gates and gave us the right information. They explained how to be an Almoner, how to be an Occupational Therapist, how to be a Physiotherapist. They gave us dreams and aspirations which we may not have been able to satisfy in the 50s and 60s, but we could pass those dreams and aspirations on to our daughters and our granddaughters.

Career Novels for Girls by Kay Clifford, Mirfield Press 2018.
ISBN 9781 5272 18109

Books set in Wartime – Recommended Reading

We have included only children's books due to space constraints. With many thanks to the following who responded to the request for recommendations: Elizabeth Allnutt, Jill Ashmore, Janice Bennett, David Bennion, Sue Berridge, Jane Chiplin, Jane Cooper, Clarissa Cridland, Sally Dore, Clare Gailans, Elizabeth Harrisson, Hilary Hartley, Averil Higginson, Sue Hodgson, Ellen Jordan, Linda Lampen, Julie Makin, Jane Medcalf, Susan Merskey, Catherine Middleton, Betula O'Neill, Barbara Penrose, Louise Plewes, Jenny Rance, Hilary Robinson; Verity Wilde, Helen-Louise Williams

An interesting observation by Elizabeth Allnutt; "The swift growing up of teenage girls seems to be a constant theme in these books, particularly in WW2. Wartime circumstances prove a rude awakening and the need to take responsibility and put childish things behind is overwhelming."

First World War

Almedingen, E.M.; *Frossia* (1943)

Brazil, Angela; *The Head Girl at the Gables* (1919). " Near the beginning there's a stirring talk from the head about how even girls can help the war effort, there's a spy in the area, funds are raised for the armed services, and poignantly, a much loved soldier cousin is killed at the front." JA

Brazil, Angela; *The Luckiest Girl in the School* (1916). "There's lots about stirring patriotic drills … but also the heroine is interested in planes, learns to drive a car while still in the 6th Form, meets a pilot and has a brother who drops out of school to enlist under age. The family attitude once they find this out is that it will "make a man of him" (!!) and no one seems horrified at all. The brother – who is a selfish, patronising character – gets wounded and of course this does make a man of him. With my 21st C attitude and knowledge, the final chapter of him being got fit enough to return to the trenches as soon as he can and describing the war as "larks" makes for uncomfortable reading but it's a good read and I like Brazil's books." JR

Breslin, Theresa; *Remembrance* (2002)

Bruce, D.F.; *Dimsie and the Jane Willard Foundation* (GGBP collection 2011)

Carter, Bruce; *B Flight* (1970)

Cowper, E.E.; *Jane in Command* (1917). "An English girl, living on the South Coast, exposes a ring of German spies." DB

Darke, Marjorie; *A Rose from Blighty* (1990).

Dowswell, Paul; *Eleven Eleven* (2012).

Farmer, Penelope; *Charlotte Sometimes*; (1969). Classic timeslip story.

Frank, Rudolf; *No Hero for the Kaiser* (1979)

Harris, John; The Martin Falconer quintet; *The Fledglings* (1971); *The Professionals* (1973); *The Victors* (1975); *The Interceptors* (1977); *The Revolutionaries* (1978). "I am still surprised these are not better known. The first three books follow Martin from basic pilot's training to becoming a commanding officer and the transformation of the RFC into the RAF. Then, very experienced while barely out of his teens, he flies in the civil war in Russia before taking part in the Mexican revolution. Action and humour and some romance, with the naïve Martin maturing over the sequence." SD

Harris, Ruth Elwin; The Quantocks Quartet - *The Silent Shore* (1986), *The Beckoning Hills* (1987), *The Dividing Sea* (1989) & *Beyond the Orchid House* (1994). "Differing viewpoints again, all female, some actually in contact with active service through nursing, some staying at home." JC "Four books set before, during and after WW1, and in the last book just before WW2, featuring four sisters and the neighbours, lives and loves in a Somerset village. Each book is told from one sister's perspective. Quite heart-breaking in parts, but captivating reading, wonderful characterisation" JM

Haverfield, E.L.; *The Girls of St Olave's* (1919).
Hooper, Mary; *Poppy* (2014) and *Poppy in the Field* (2015).
Kenyon, Edith C.; *Pickles, A Red Cross Heroine* (1916). "Pickles (real name Joan) is seventeen, qualified as a nurse, but her father forbids her to go to France to join the Red Cross with her older sisters. She is determined however, and the book is an account of her rather unlikely adventures. She gets to France, for example, by hitching a lift in the plane of a friend of her brother's, who just happens to have landed nearby, in the hope of persuading the brother to be his observer. Pickles goes instead. Later on, she uses her medical knowledge to drug a whole room-full of German officers, to help her father escape. Interestingly, as well as coloured plates accompanying the story, there are b&w photographs of casualty stations and hospitals." DB
Little, Jean; *His Banner Over Me* (1995). "Missionary family returns to Canada from Taiwan. Parents return. WW1 arrives, troubles ensue." EA
Lovelace, Maud Hart; *Betsy and the Great World* (1952), *Betsy's Wedding* (1955). WWI from an American point of view. Based on author's own letters home.
Marchant, Bessie; *Molly Angel's Adventures* (1915). "This is the story of three English children, aged thirteen, ten and eight, who are stranded in Belgium when the Germans invade, and how they find their way home." DB
Marchant, Bessie; *A Transport Girl in France* (1920).
McCutcheon, Elsie; *Summer of the Zeppelin* (1983). "Country story – Elvira's father at war, teacher gone to make munitions, POW's working in the fields. But it turns out to be a very memorable summer" EA
Montgomery, L.M.; *Rilla of Ingleside* (1920). Canadian home front "This is now seen as a very significant account." SD "It made me laugh and cry."JCh
Moore, Dorothea; *Wanted. An English Girl* (written in 1915) "Subtitled *The Adventures of an English Schoolgirl in Germany.* About a girl who is sent to be a companion to a German girl but gets caught up in the war. Very descriptive, sometimes rather too much detail - gruesome in parts." JM
Morpurgo, Michael; *War Horse* (1982).
Newbery, Linda; First World War trilogy, *Some Other War* (1990), *The Kind Ghosts* (1991), *The Wearing of the Green* (1992)
Parkinson, Siobhan; *No Peace for Amelia* (1994) "Irish. Sets WW1 in context of Easter Rising and Quaker boyfriend who goes off to fight. Interesting! Sequel to "Amelia" which I have never been able to find." EA
Peyton, K.M.; *The Flambards trilogy* (1967-69). Books 2 and 3 include WWI.
Saunders, Kate; *Five Children on the Western Front* (2014). "What happens to E. Nesbit's young adults when the Psammead appears again." EA
Seredy, Kate; *The Good Master* (1937) & *The Singing Tree* (1939) "They are set on the Hungarian plains. The first tells the story of Jansci and Kate as they grow up just before WW1 and how they cope when the outbreak of war takes the 'good master' off to war. *The Singing Tree* is a sequel and covers the finding of Kate's father in a field hospital (with amnesia). The title comes from the only thing existing in the war torn landscape which is a barren tree, but all the birds take shelter in it and so it becomes a 'singing tree'." HH

Streatfeild, Noel; *A Vicarage Family* (1963). Fictionalised autobiography. "This highlighted when war broke out in 1914 and the effect on family members - based on her own experiences." JMe.
Symons, Geraldine; *Mademoiselle* (1973). "August 1914 - Pansy and her friend Atalanta are on holiday in Paris. When the school Mademoiselle began creeping out at night and acting mysteriously, it became quite an interesting and patriotic duty to do a little sleuthing of their own." CM
Talbot, Ethel; *Peggy's Last Term* (1920). "Boarding school / guides on East Anglia coast." EH
Wilson, Barbara Ker; *The Lovely Summer* (1960).

Second World War
Alington, Gabriel; *Evacuee* (1988)
Allan, Mabel Esther; *Tomorrow is a Lovely Day* (1979). "15 year old heroine lives through London blitz but falls foul of a flying bomb and goes and works for a school in the Chilterns." EA
Allan, Mabel Esther; *A Strange Enchantment* (1982). Land army.
Anderson, Margaret J.; *Searching for Shona* (1978). "At the start of WW2, children are being evacuated. Shona is being sent to the country, her friend Marjorie to Canada to relatives she's never seen. "Let's change places" said Marjorie to Shona. "No one will ever know". So they switch identities and the story begins..." CM "About two girls, one rich and one from an orphanage, who swap identities when they are evacuated during the war. A delightful book about the consequences of an impulsive action." JM
Avi; *Don't You Know There's a War On?* (2001). Howie in New York.
Barne, Kitty; *Family Footlights* (1939). "Children put on show to raise money to retrieve a refugee's violin." BP
Barne, Kitty; *Visitors From London* (1940). "Same family as above and the impact of evacuees on an insular rural area." BP
Barne, Kitty; May I Keep Dogs? (1941) "A family all doing their bit for the war and the youngest runs a boarding kennel for absentee dog owners. Father absent in forces." BP
Barne, Kitty; *We'll Meet in England* (1942). "Teenagers escape from Norway in a small sailing boat and pick up a ditched RAF pilot en route." BP
Barne, Kitty; *Three and A Pigeon* (1944). "In new home (after being bombed out), find refugee boy and pigeons being used for the black market." BP
Barne, Kitty; *In the Same Boat* (1945). English and Polish 12year-old girls.
Barne, Kitty; *Musical Honours* (1947). "Family reunion with POW father and how they all cope with peacetime demands." BP
Bawden, Nina; *Carrie's War* (1973)
Benary, Margot; *A Time to Love* (1962). "German girl at school." EH
Benary, Margot; *Dangerous Spring* (1961).
Boyne, John; *The Boy in the Striped Pyjamas* (2006)
Brent-Dyer, Elinor M.; *The Chalet School in Exile* (1940), *The Chalet School Goes To It* (1941), *The Highland Twins at the Chalet School* (1942).
Bruce, D.F.; *Toby of Tibbs Cross* (1942). Toby becomes a land girl.
Bruce, D.F.; *Nancy Calls the Tune* (1944).
Bruce, D.F.; *Dimsie Carries On* (1941).
Burton, Hester; *In Spite of All Terror* (1968) "The title is taken from one of Churchill's rousing speeches. Liz, from the East End of London, and the

cultivated Brutons on whom she is billeted, live in a fog of mutual misunderstanding, until they gradually work out that even those who are different can have admirable qualities; culminates in Dunkirk. This was one of my childhood discoveries and has remained a huge favourite." SD
Carter, Bruce; *The Children who Stayed Behind*. (1964) (Originally *The Kidnapping of Kensington* (a rabbit), 1959). "It's a fantasy - what would happen if the Germans had invaded the south coast? And two sets of children got left behind to ramble round a deserted Brighton on their own. I really liked it - the contrast between the wild Foulsham family and the well-behaved Hartfords and Brighton, where we visited quite often as a family day trip, with nobody in it." EA
Chapman, Michael; *The Riddle of the Caves* (2014) "The Frobisher family, two brothers and a sister, father in the Navy, move to Dorset with another school friend and become involved in catching a spy on the cliffs and caves near their house. Full of suspense, very descriptive, lovely characters." JM
Cooper, Michelle; The Montmaray Journals; *A Brief History of Montmaray* (2008), *The FitzOsbornes in Exile* (2010), *The FitzOsbornes at War* (2012).
Cooper, Susan; *Dawn of Fear* (1970)
Courtney, G; *The Denehurst Secret Service* (1940), *Well Done, Denehurst!* (1941)
Crompton, Richmal; William titles, eg *William and ARP* (1939), *William and the Evacuees* (1940), *William Does His Bit* (1941); *William Carries On* (1942)
Dennison, Dorothy; *Corrie and Co* (1948)
Donaldson, Margaret; *Journey Into War* (1979)
Dowswell, Paul; *Bomber* (2015).
Enright, Elizabeth; *The Four-Storey Mistake* (1942).
French, Jackie; *Hitler's Daughter* (1999).
Frow, Marion; The *Darcy Family* series: *The Intelligence Corps & Anna* (1944), *The Intelligence Corps Saves the Island* (1946), *The Submerged Cave* (1947), *Four Stowaways & Anna* (1947), *Castle Adventure* (1949), *Five Robinson Crusoes* (1950) *& A Ghost for Christmas* (1951). "The first 2 are set during the war, in London, then moving to Wales for safety. The Darcy family are four children and their dog, Anna, nursing mother and forces father. Written during wartime, very authentic. Charming series and lovely illustrations." JM
Gallico, Paul; *The Snow Goose* (1941). "I absolutely love it." BO'N
Gardam, Jane; *A Long Way from Verona* (1971). "Jessica strives for individuality against background of a penniless curate father's household and girls' day school." EA
Gleitzman, Morris; the Felix and Zelda books; *Once* (2006); *Then* (2009); *Now* (2010), *After* (2012), *Soon* (2015).
Handford, Nourma; *Three Came from Britain* (1945). "One of my two favourite overseas evacuee stories (the other is *I go by Sea, I Go by Land*)." EJ
Harris, Mary K.; *Gretel at St Bride's* (1941).
Hartnett, Sonya; *The Children of the King* (2012). "Family of three evacuated to the country in WW2 encounter the ghosts of the Princes in the Tower." EA
Hautzig, Esther; *The Endless Steppe* (1968) "Poland and Siberia. Polish family life in war and transportation to camps." EA
Heneghan, James; *Wish Me Luck* (1997). Jamie evacuated to Canada.
Holm, Anne; *I am David***;** (1963, trans. from Danish)
Hughes, Dean; *Four-Four-Two* (2016). Two second-generation Japanese Americans enlist in the 442nd Regiment.

Hughes, Shirley; *The Lion and the Unicorn* (1998). "This a large sized picture book, with beautiful and atmospheric illustrations in Shirely Hughes' inimitable style. The story is simple but telling – young Lenny, evacuated to the country, learns that being brave is not the same as not being afraid." SD
Hughes, Shirley; *Hero on a Bicycle* (2012). This is actually the author's first novel, set in wartime Florence where Paolo tries to help escaped prisoners.
Hughes, Shirley; *Whistling in the Dark* (2015). Her second novel, using her wartime memories, featuring the blitz in Liverpool.
Iturbe, Antonio; *The Librarian of Auschwitz* (2012). Based on a real child, a 14 year old girl guards 8 precious books.
Kay, Mara; *Storm Warning* UK title (1976), *In Face of Danger* USA title (1976)
Kerr, Judith; *Out of the Hitler Time* trilogy; *When Hitler Stole Pink Rabbit* (1971); *The Other Way Round* (1975); *A Small Person Far Away* (1978).
King, Clive; *The Sound of Propellers* (1986). "Murugan from India finds strange goings-on at the Shorts aircraft factory near his boarding school. Beautifully intelligent, believable writing." SD
Koehn, Ilse; *Mischling, Second Degree* (1977)
Kuenzler, Lou; *The Return of the Railway Children* (2018). Edie evacuated to Aunt Roberta and Uncle Peter.
Lasky, Kathryn; *Night Witches – A Novel of WWII* (2017)
Lewis, Lorna; *Tea and Hot Bombs* (1943) "About the mobile tea canteens that drive to bombed areas to provide tea and food and comfort." JM
Lewis, Lorna; *Feud in the Factory* (1944) "About women working in a wartime factory. Both written during wartime, very authentic, very descriptive." JM
Lingard, Joan; *The File on Fraulein Berg* (1980)
Magorian, Michelle; *Goodnight, Mister Tom* (1981) "This is very emotional about the tribulations of a young boy evacuated from a London slum to the country and his relationship with the older crusty Mr Tom." JMe
Magorian, Michelle; *A Little Love Song* (1991).
Magorian, Michelle; *Back Home* (1984). "An emotional rollercoaster." JCh
Matthewman, Phyllis; *Jill on the Land* (1942)
Matthewman, Phyllis; *Timber Girl* (1944).
Mitchelhill, Barbara; *Run Rabbit Run* (2011). "Children of Conscientious Objector father on run from the Police and try to stay together as a family. Part set in Whiteway - alternative "hippy" community still in existence. Really liked the bits about Whiteway and CO father. " EA
Mitchison, Naomi; *The Rib of the Green Umbrella* (1960) "Young Piero smuggles cartridges to the partisans now that the Germans have changed from being friends to occupiers of his hill town. A real feeling of Italy." SD
Morpurgo, Michael; *Waiting for Anya* (1990)
Osborne, William; *Hitler's Angel* (2012).
Pardoe, M; *Bunkle Began It* (1942)
Pearson, Kit; The *Guests of War* trilogy; *The Sky is Falling* (1989), *Looking at the Moon* (1991), *The Lights Go on Again* (1993). Norah and her little brother Gavin are evacuated to Canada.
Plowman, Stephanie; *Three Lives for the Czar* (1969) and *My Kingdom for a Grave* (1970). "Very powerful stories; young Andrei Hamilton growing up at court during the 1905 uprising and the years before and during WWI." SD
Rae, Gwynedd; *Mary Plain in Wartime* (1942) "Not to be missed!" EH
Rees, David; *The Exeter Blitz* (1978)

Reiss, Johanna; *The Upstairs Room* (1972) "Based on the author's own experiences of being Jewish in occupied Holland." SD
Richter, Hans Peter; *Friedrich* (1961)
Salisbury, Graham; Prisoners of the Empire series; *Under the Blood-Red Sun* (1994), *Eyes of the Emperor* (2005), *House of the Red Fish* (2006), *Hunt for the Bamboo Rat* (2014). Four different takes on the clash of cultures and national identities created for young Japanese-Americans in WWII.
Saville, Malcolm; *Mystery at Witchend* (1943).
Seredy, Kate; *The Chestry Oak* (1948) (Hungary/USA)
Serraillier, Ian; *The Silver Sword* (1956) (Poland/Switzerland)
Smith, Emma, *Maidens' Trip* (1948). Lightly fictionalised account of her own wartime experiences working on the Grand Union Canal.
Smith, Madge, S.; *Peggy Speeds the Plough* (1941). "Peggy is a Land Girl, who has volunteered for farm work, rather than spend a final year at school. Has some interesting accounts of farmers being sued by parents for large sums of money, when evacuees are hurt on the farm, and this is no fault of the farmer. Peggy manages to get a promise from the parents of her farmer's evacuees, not to take unreasonable action if the children get hurt." DB
Stockum, Hilda van; *The Winged Watchman* (1964), *The Borrowed House* (1975)
Streatfeild, Noel; *The Children of Primrose Lane* (1941). *Party Frock* (1946)
Streatfeild, Noel; *Curtain Up* (1944). "I love the descriptions of blitz-ravaged London, and the privations caused by the war – the problems with getting clothing, food and suitable presents (and attaché cases!)" JCh
Suhl, Yuri; *Uncle Misha's Partisans* (1973)
Swindells, Robert; *Blitzed* (2002), timeslip story, and *Shrapnel* (2009).
Temperley, Alan; *Murdo's War* (1988)
Terlouw, Jan; *Winter in Wartime* (1975). Dutch winter under occupation.
Thor, Annika; *A Faraway Island* (1996), *The Lily Pond* (1997), *Deep Sea* (1998), *Open Sea* (1999). "With the ever-growing threat of Nazi persecution, Jewish Steffi and Nelli Steiner's parents decide to send them from Vienna to live on a remote Swedish island while they make arrangements for the whole family to emigrate to the USA. Steffi promises her father that she will always look after her younger sister but the first problem she encounters is that they are separated and sent to live with different families as no-one is able to take them both. Yet while Steffi struggles to fit in with 'Aunt Marta' and 'Uncle Evert', Nelli settles with her own family immediately and soon adapts to her new life. Letters are exchanged between Vienna and Sweden but it soon becomes apparent that the move to the USA is not going to happen as quickly as hoped. *Open Sea* is only available in English on Kindle although HLW wrote her own full translation from French into English in 2018." SB & HLW
Toksvig, Sandi; *Hitler's Canary* (2005). A Danish boy's war.
Travers, P.L.; *I Go By Sea, I Go By Land* (1941). Sabrina evacuated to the USA.
Treadgold, Mary; *We Couldn't Leave Dinah* (1941).
Trease, Geoffrey; *Tomorrow is a Stranger.* "Set in Guernsey during the German occupation, from a teenage boy and girl's perspective. Full of suspense and GT's wonderful writing." JM
Trease, Geoffrey; *The Arpino Assignment* (1988)
Trease, Geoffrey; *Black Night, Red Morning* (1944). "A Buchanesque thriller - the Soviet resistance to the Nazi invasion." SD
Walsh, Jill Paton; *The Dolphin Crossing* (1967). "Two boys, a boat, Dunkirk."

Walsh, Jill Paton; *Fireweed* (1969).
Watson, Victor; Paradise Barn series; *Paradise Barn* (2009), *Operation Blackout* (2015), *The Deeping Secrets* (2011), *Hidden Lies* (2012), *Everyone a Stranger* (2013). Victor gave a fascinating talk about writing these at the 2016 conference (see Conference Papers 2016).
Westall, Robert; *The Machine Gunners* (1975). "My favourite (I used to borrow the cassette tapes from the library fairly frequently)." VW
Westall, Robert; *Blitzcat* (1989)
Whitehead, Elizabeth; *Adventurous Exile* (1946). "My mum chose it for me from the stock of braille books, and I stayed awake all the first night of the school holidays (no light needed of course) to finish it. I re-read it often. A really exciting story with only a small number of girls, eight I think, who are caught in occupied France where they had (strange timing) gone on a school trip. And nuns, which did not strike me as unusual at the time, since I was also at a convent boarding-school." CG
Wilson, Barbara Ker; *Last Year's Broken Toys*. "About a group of friends in a small industrial town and their lives, loves and plans for the future, and what they do in the war. Full of suspense and not a happy ending for some." JM

Other Wars
Troy
Geras, Adele; *Troy* (2000)
Green, Roger Lancelyn; *The Luck of Troy* (1961)
Treece, Henry; *The Windswept City* (1967)

Peloponnesian Wars
McGregor, Iona; *The Snake and the Olive* (1974)
Plowman, Stephanie; *The Road to Sardis* (1966)
Plowman, Stephanie; *The Leaping Song* (1975)

Roman Empire
Mitchison, Naomi; *When the Bough Breaks* (1924)
Sutcliff, Rosemary; *The Eagle of the Ninth* (1954)
Treece, Henry; *Legions of the Eagle* (1954)

Norman Invasion and Aftermath
Lewis, Hilda; *Harold was My King* (1968)
Polland, Madeline; *To Kill a King* (1970)
Sutcliff, Rosemary; *The Shield Ring* (1956)
Treece, Henry; *Man with a Sword* (1961) About Hereward the Wake

The Civil War
Brent-Dyer, Elinor M; *Elizabeth the Gallant* (1935)
Marryat, Captain; *The Children of the New Forest* (1847)
Oxenham, Elsie J; *The Girls of Gwynfa* (1924)
Softly, Barbara; *Plain Jane* (1961), *Place Mill* (1962), *A Stone in a Pool* (1965)
Sutcliff, Rosemary; *Simon* (1953)
Sutcliff, Rosemary; *The Rider of the White Horse* (1959)
Willard, Barbara; *Harrow and Harvest* (1974).
Yonge, C.M; *Under the Storm, or Steadfast's Charge* (1887)
"Three Civil War books [*Marryat, Sutcliff, Yonge*] written in different periods provide interestingly different viewpoints and attitudes." JC

Napoleonic Wars
Burton, Hester; *Castors Away* (1962). "Tom Henchman with Nelson and his sister Nell frustrated at home in Norfolk. Wonderfully characterised." SD
Overton, Jenny; *The Ship from Simnel Street* (1986)
Redmayne, John; *Substitute General* (1965), *Redcoat Spy* (1964), *The Night Riders* (1967). "3 stories of Major Peter Maclean and his feisty Spanish wife Cristina, childhood library favourites. They still stand up well now." SD
Styles, Showell; *Midshipman Quinn* (1956), *Quinn of the Fury* (1958), *Midshipman Quinn and Denise the Spy* (1961), *Midshipman Quinn Wins Through* (1961), *Quinn at Trafalgar* (1965), "These are a sort of junior Hornblower, very successfully done – very entertaining." SD
Trease, Geoffrey; *Violet for Bonaparte* (1976)

Russian Decembrist Rising
Kay, Mara; *The Youngest Lady-in-Waiting* (1969)

Italian Unification
Trease, Geoffrey; *Follow My Black Plume* (1963), *A Thousand for Sicily* (1964).

Taiping Rebellion
Paterson, Katherine; *Rebels of the Heavenly Kingdom* (1983)

American Civil War
Alcott, L.M; *Little Women* (1868)
Brenaman, Miriam; *Evvy's Civil War* (2002) "Feisty heroine who will not conform to Southern belle behaviour norms." EA
Fleischman, Paul; *Bull Run* (1993)
Hunt, Irene; *Across Five Aprils* (1964)
Lunn, Janet; *The Root Cellar* (1981)

Malaysian Campaign
Marks, J.M; *Ayo Gurkha!* (1971)

The Carey Series by Ronald Welch - Clarissa Cridland
The 'Carey Series' is a loosely connected series of 13 books, featuring members of the Carey family through the ages, fighting in different wars. These books are a wonderful way to find out about various conflicts, from the point of view of someone fighting. Because of the Carey connection there is also a good series element. Ronald Welch didn't write the series in order, and although it is best read that way, it is perfectly possible to dip in and out.

Knight Crusader (1954) – the Crusades (1185)
Bowman of Crécy (1966) – Battle of Crécy (1356)
Sun of York (1970) – Wars of the Roses (1469 – 1470)
The Galleon (1971) – Spain, Babington Plot (1583)
The Hawk (1967) – Spain, Mary Queen of Scots (1584)
For the King (1961) – English Civil War (1642 – 1645)
Captain of Dragoons (1956) - Battle of Blenheim (1704)
Mohawk Valley (1958) – British / French war in Canada (1755 – 1759)
Escape from France (1960) - French Revolution (1791)
Captain of Foot (1959) - War with Spain (1810 – 1812)
Nicholas Carey (1963) - Italy, France, Crimean War (1853 – 1855)
Ensign Carey (1976) - India, esp Mutiny (1853 – 1857)
Tank Commander (1972) – WWI (1914 – 1918)